Sam Maverick's Trail

SAM MAVERICK'S TRAIL

*The Story of the First American Exploration
of the Texas-Mexico Border*

DANIEL McNEEL LANE, MD, PhD

SUNSTONE PRESS
SANTA FE

© 2017 by Daniel McNeel Lane, MD, PhD
All Rights Reserved.
No part of this book may be reproduced in any form or by any electronic or mechanical means including information storage and retrieval systems without permission in writing from the publisher, except by a reviewer who may quote brief passages in a review.

Sunstone books may be purchased for educational, business, or sales promotional use. For information please write: Special Markets Department, Sunstone Press, P.O. Box 2321, Santa Fe, New Mexico 87504-2321.

Book and cover design › Vicki Ahl
Body typeface › Book Antiqua
Printed on acid-free paper
∞
eBook 978-1-61139-501-3

Library of Congress Cataloging-in-Publication Data

Names: Lane, Daniel McNeel, 1936- author.
Title: Sam Maverick's trail : the first American exploration of the Texas-Mexico border / by Daniel McNeel Lane, MD, PhD.
Description: Santa Fe : Sunstone Press, 2016. | Includes bibliographical references.
Identifiers: LCCN 2016052901 (print) | LCCN 2016059187 (ebook) | ISBN 9781632931702 (softcover : alkaline paper) | ISBN 9781611395013
Subjects: LCSH: Maverick, Samuel Augustus, 1803-1870--Travel--Texas. | Texas--Description and travel. | Mexican-American Border Region--Description and travel. | Mexican-American Border Region--Discovery and exploration. | Frontier and pioneer life--Texas. | Trails--Texas--History--19th century. | Borderlands--Texas--History--19th century. | Pioneers--Texas--Biography. | Explorers--Texas--Biography.
Classification: LCC F391 .L33 2016 (print) | LCC F391 (ebook) | DDC 976.4/35102092--dc23
LC record available at https://lccn.loc.gov/2016052901

SUNSTONE PRESS IS COMMITTED TO MINIMIZING OUR ENVIRONMENTAL IMPACT ON THE PLANET. THE PAPER USED IN THIS BOOK IS FROM RESPONSIBLY MANAGED FORESTS. OUR PRINTER HAS RECEIVED CHAIN OF CUSTODY (COC) CERTIFICATION FROM: THE FOREST STEWARDSHIP COUNCIL™ (FSC®), PROGRAMME FOR THE ENDORSEMENT OF FOREST CERTIFICATION™ (PEFC™), AND THE SUSTAINABLE FORESTRY INITIATIVE® (SFI®). THE FSC® COUNCIL IS A NON-PROFIT ORGANIZATION, PROMOTING THE ENVIRONMENTALLY APPROPRIATE, SOCIALLY BENEFICIAL AND ECONOMICALLY VIABLE MANAGEMENT OF THE WORLD'S FORESTS. FSC® CERTIFICATION IS RECOGNIZED INTERNATIONALLY AS A RIGOROUS ENVIRONMENTAL AND SOCIAL STANDARD FOR RESPONSIBLE FOREST MANAGEMENT.

WWW.SUNSTONEPRESS.COM
SUNSTONE PRESS / POST OFFICE BOX 2321 / SANTA FE, NM 87504-2321 /USA
(505) 988-4418 / ORDERS ONLY (800) 243-5644 / FAX (505) 988-1025

Contents

Preface / 7

1 / Background / 11

Spanish Exploration and Settlement of Texas _____ 11
U.S. Presidents and Rights To Texas _____ 13
Mexican Governance of Texas _____ 15
Revolution Against Mexico by Republic of Texas _____ 17
Annexation of Texas Republic _____ 19
Political Unrest in Mexico: 1836–1845 _____ 23
The Mexican-American War _____ 24
Treaty of Guadalupe Hidalgo _____ 27
    Peace Treaty and Its Final Approval _____ 27
    Rio Grande As Texas-Mexico Border _____ 28
American Obligations Under Article XI of the Treaty _____ 29
The "Apacheria" and the "Comancheria" _____ 30

2 / Objectives and Members of 1848 Pioneer Expedition / 35

Objectives of 1848 Chihuahua-El Paso Pioneer Expedition _____ 35
Major Groups Involved _____ 38
Leaders of the Expedition _____ 40

3 / Rendezvous at Las Moras Springs / The Edwards Plateau / 47

San Antonio to Las Moras Springs _____ 47
The Old Spanish Missions _____ 57

4 / Westward to La Junta De Los Rios / The River Canyon Country / 61

Las Moras Springs To Lower Pecos River Canyon _____ 61
Never A Despoblado by Joe Labadie _____ 72
Up the Rio Grande to Sanderson Canyon _____ 77
Meeting with Mescalero Indians _____ 82
The Discovery in Sanderson Canyon by Louis Aulbach _____ 85
A Band of Texans Explores the Big Bend _____ 90
Through Mexico to La Junta de los Rios _____ 97
Fort Leaton _____ 101

5 / Return East to Home / Alamitos Creek and Pecos River Valley / 107

Presidio del Norte to Horsehead Crossing _____ 107
"Seventy-four miles lost down the Pecos" _____ 114
Horsehead Crossing to Granger Draw _____ 117
Expedition Separates For Return _____ 122
   Highsmith's Rangers to Castell _____ 123
   Hays/Maverick to Las Moras Springs _____ 124
   Leona River Back to San Antonio _____ 128

6 / Second Exploration of Texas-Mexico Border: / 133

Reconnaissance to El Paso del Norte by Whiting/Smith _____ 133
San Saba River to Davis Mountains _____ 133
Fort Leaton to El Paso del Norte _____ 135
New Route Back From El Paso del Norte _____ 137

7 / The Border After Signing of Treaty / 139

Ratification by the U.S. Senate and President _____ 139
Ratification by the Mexican Congress _____ 139
Completion of the Hays Expedition's Goals _____ 141
   Finding Route for San Antonio-El Paso Wagon Road _____ 141
   Transfer of Border Protection to U.S. Army _____ 141
   Frontier Forts Along the Road to El Paso _____ 142

Epilogue / 144

Methods Used to Locate Trail of 1848 Expedition / 146
Article XI of the Treaty of Guadalupe Hidalgo / 154
Approximate GPS Locations of 1848 Campsites / 156

Afterword / 160

References / 163

Preface

Despite the exploration's economic, military and political significance, the route of the 1848 Chihuahua-El Paso Pioneer Expedition's (Hays) exploration of the Texas-Mexico border had never been accurately defined following the return of Jack Hays and Sam Maverick (SAM) to San Antonio in December 1848. As I stood on the western bank of the Pecos River at Horsehead Crossing in 1998, where the Pioneer Expedition forded the river on its way home exactly 150 years ago to the day, I could not imagine how the Expedition's members had managed to survive traveling through the unbelievably vast and barren lands of far West Texas. The Pecos River was no longer "forty feet wide and twenty feet deep," as described in Sam Maverick's journal about the Pioneer Expedition,[1] but just a trickle of water in the riverbed below me. Despite the brevity of SAM's journal, it is and was the only complete record of the 1848 Pioneer Expedition's route from San Antonio de Bexar to La Junta de los Rios and their return home.

Stimulated by my visit to Horsehead Crossing, I undertook a careful review of SAM's journal and, while living in western Texas not far from Horsehead Crossing, spent several years of research seeking the Expedition's original trail as described in Maverick's journal. By utilizing resources which had not been used in the past, such as 3D topographic computer maps, (see "Methods Used to Locate Trail of 1848 Expedition"), an approximate route of the original trail based on the campsite locations described in SAM's journal was finally located. Using that data, my cousin, Jim Keller, a professional photographer, and I began re-exploration of the original 1848 trail in early 2004 with the intent to confirm the 1848 route with photographs. Much of the re-exploration was completed under unusual climatic conditions for the TransPecos/Big Bend region, that is, during a year when rainfall had been greater than in almost 50 years. The changes produced by the heavy rains were most obvious during our first trip to Horsehead Crossing where the power of the Pecos River flood waters was demonstrated. Prior to that trip, a flood down the river had washed away the fences and gate as well as most of the vegetation along both banks of the river that I had seen during my

March, 1998 trip. The area around Horsehead Crossing was covered with a deep layer of white sandy clay that had re-landscaped the river's course. Driving in the tenacious and deep wet clay made it easy to understand why so many horses had drowned in the quicksand, leaving only their skulls to give the crossing its name. The changes produced by the 2004 flood served as an example of the conditions that future travelers crossing the Pecos River would have to face as they passed through far West Texas.

Our primary goal was to re-explore and photograph the trail of the first Texans to cross the *terra incognita* along the state's new border with Mexico, as defined by the 1848 Treaty of Guadalupe Hidalgo between Mexico and the United States. We started our re-exploration of the 1848 Expedition's trail in San Antonio and passed through the Texas Hill Country to Las Moras Springs. From there we followed the Rio Grande from the Devils River to La Junta de los Rios (now Ojinaja, Chihuahua). After a visit to Fort Leaton, we turned northeast along Alamitos Creek to the Pecos River Valley, part of which would become the wagon route between Chihuahua and San Antonio. Returning home across the Edwards Plateau completed the re-exploration of the Hays Expedition's 1,300 mile exploration. Thus, the 1848 Expedition's travels through America's newly acquired *terra incognita* provided the first description of the incredibly complex terrain of far West Texas.

Without minimizing the importance of what the Expedition had achieved, it should be noted that the 1848 Pioneer Expedition explored lands that were a *terra incognita* only to Anglo-Americans. Many expeditions from New Spain had passed through the region over hundreds of years, thus the lands were no *terra incognita* to the Spaniards. However, the Spanish description of the lands as *La Tierra Despoblada* was also incorrect since indigenous tribes had lived in and traveled through the region for over 10,000 years. Despite the Pioneer Expedition's major goal of exploring the region from San Antonio to Chihuahua and El Paso, one of its most significant findings may have been learning that America's new lands along the Rio Grande were not and had not been a true *despoblado* for centuries. Besides finding the trails, river crossings and campfires of indigenous tribes, the Pioneer Expedition also found evidence of early human inhabitants in the form of Rock Art painted thousands of years earlier. Even today, in the 21st Century, scientists in many fields pursue more information about the ancient peoples who lived in Texas for thousands of years.

Finally, it is important to emphasize that the Chihuahua-El Paso Pioneer Expedition of 1848, the first American exploration of western Texas, was conceived and successfully completed by veteran Texas frontiersmen, many of whom had been Mounted Texas Volunteers in the war with Mexico. After the Expedition's 1848 return from western Texas, the United States Army expanded its exploration of the Texas-Mexico border with the assistance of several members from the Pioneer Expedition. The second reconnaissance by Lieutenants Whiting and Smith in 1849 completed the border exploration from Presidio del Norte up to El Paso del Norte while they sought a route along the Rio Grande for a wagon road to El Paso. Those early expeditions along the Mexico-Texas border provided the foundation on which subsequent Army expeditions would build roads to El Paso. Today, in the 21st Century, most of the road from San Antonio to El Paso still follows the trails of the 1848 and 1849 expeditions.

Note: Because this story is based on the daily journal of Sam Maverick, major sources of data are referenced in chronological sequence as they appear in the text.

— Daniel McNeel Lane, MD, PhD

1
BACKGROUND

Spanish Exploration and Settlement of Texas

The original *entradas*, or expeditions, to settle Texas were organized as a joint effort between the Roman Catholic Church and the Royal Government of Spain. The original purpose was to establish Spanish communities under the protection of Spanish soldiers where the native Indian population could be converted to Christianity. The mission-presidio system used by the Spaniards was based on establishing Catholic missions for settlers and the clergy, usually Franciscan friars, near presidios from which a garrison of Spanish soldiers protected the missions from hostile tribes opposing their settlement.

The series of events which followed can be summarized by stating that the efforts by the Roman Catholic missions to convert the members of the local tribes met with transient success at best (2). The initial problems began with the Spanish missionaries trying to convert members of friendly indigenous tribes, collectively called the Tejas. Unfortunately, becoming friends of the Tejas turned their enemies, especially the Lipan Apaches, against the Spanish missionaries and presidio soldiers. In the 1750s, peaceful relations with the native tribes became even more difficult to maintain when Comanche tribes, called the Nortenos, moved south into central Texas. The Comanches forced the Apaches out of their lands toward the west and frequently attacked the Catholic missions protected by Spanish presidios.

On August 7, 1764, King Charles III commissioned the Marques de Rubi to inspect the presidios on the northern frontier of New Spain after complaints about their cost to Spain. The Marques spent almost two years visiting and inspecting the many Spanish missions and presidios from California to Louisiana. What he learned was that the missions' attempts to Christianize the indigenous tribal members had failed in Texas. After Rubi completed his inspection of Texas in November 1767, the Marques made several recommendations that would ultimately have a major impact on Spain's role in the governance of Texas.

The conclusion of Rubi's 1767 report was that the system combining Catholic missions with Spanish presidios had not been successful, not only in converting native tribes to Christianity but also in protecting Spanish settlers from raids by the hostile Indian tribes. Rubi was impressed with the success of only two presidio-mission sites in Texas. San Antonio with its presidio and five successful missions was the most impressive of the Texas presidios. The other site was Presidio La Bahia with its two missions, both of which had Indian residents. His recommendation was that Presidio La Bahia be the eastern end of a line of presidios stretching from the Gulf of California to the Gulf of Mexico.

Despite Rubi's recommendations being ignored for four years, Presidio San Saba was abandoned in 1770 and its troops moved down to the missions in the Nueces River Canyon. During the following years, soldiers stationed in the missions on the Nueces River were withdrawn to other new presidios and the missions closed. On September 10, 1772, the "New Regulations for Presidios" ordered by the Spanish king confirmed the recommendations made by Marques de Rubi.[2] All Texas missions, except San Antonio and La Bahia, were to be abandoned with San Antonio to become the capital of Texas. A new Indian policy was developed to improve relations with the northern tribes against the Apaches. After receiving the King's orders on May 18, 1773, the Texas Governor, as ordered by Commandant O'Conor, transferred the residents and soldiers from eastern Texas to San Antonio. Of the abandoned settlements, only Nacogdoches, built on the former site of a mission, was re-established later by a group of former residents despite the Royal Edict to survive as the only Spanish community in eastern Texas.

Following his departure from Texas in November, 1767, Rubi inspected the presidio at San Juan Bautista and found that it was effectively fighting off Apaches raids. Instead of closing that site, he recommended that the Rio Grande presidio be enlarged and included in the northern line of defense with Spanish presidios extending from the Gulf of California to the mouth of Guadalupe River. Santa Fe and San Antonio would be the only Spanish settlements north of the presidios protected by Spanish soldiers. All of the East Texas presidios were abandoned, leaving only the presidios at San Antonio and La Bahia. Rubi's final suggestion was that Spain form an alliance with the northern tribes (such as the Comanches) to exterminate the Apaches, reflecting his ignorance of the Comanches' power and influence.

By 1778 the northern line of seventeen presidios from Texas to

California had been established and garrisoned with thousands of soldiers to defend New Spain from Indian attacks. By 1782 completion of the new presidios had ended the mission-presidio alliance between the Roman Catholic Church and the Spanish government in Texas. Unfortunately, the presidential defensive system to prevent Indian depredations in New Spain proved to be as ineffective as the mission-presidio system had been.

A new and greater problem for Spain developed with the American declaration of independence from England three years after the evacuation by Spain. After its war of independence, a peace treaty with England was finally ratified by the U.S. Congress in January, 1784. Peace with England was followed by France's re-acquisition of Louisiana in 1800 and its subsequent sale in 1803 to the United States under President Jefferson. The birth of the new nation created an even greater problem for Spain. Besides having to defend its northern frontier against hostile Indian tribes, New Spain had a new aggressively and rapidly growing nation on its eastern border.

Despite agreement on several disputes between Spain and the United States in the Transcontinental Boundary of 1819, the treaty was not approved immediately by Spain. Because of objections raised by Secretary of State Adams, the Spanish King did not agree to the Transcontinental Treaty until two years later on February 22, 1821.[3]

By that time, the Spanish government in Texas had already given permission to Moses Austin to settle three hundred families in Texas.[4, p. 240] The colony was established by his son, Stephen F. Austin, who organized the settlement after his father's unexpected death. The "Old Three Hundred," the name given to the original members of Austin's colony, included Daniel McNeel, this author's ancestor, as well as his older brother, John, who settled in Brazoria County where they were successful planters for many years.

U.S. Presidents and Rights to Texas

President Thomas Jefferson believed that when the United States purchased the Louisiana Purchase in 1803, its limits extended westward to the Rio Grande del Norte. In support of that viewpoint, John Melish wrote the following in the 1816 book that accompanied his map of the United States:[5, p21] "In the year 1684, La Salle sailed from France, with a small squadron, for the purpose of establishing a colony on the Mississippi; but missing the mouth of the river, he reached the bay of St. Louis, called by the Spanish, and marked on the map, the Bay of St. Joseph. Here three of his vessels were cast away. The greatest part of the men and supplies were saved; but he himself was taken ill. Upon his recovery, he took possession of the country, formed a settlement, and built a fort, which is now known as Fort Matagorda. At this time there were no other settlements in that part of the country, so that the right of France became unquestionable; and all of the subsequent settlements of Spain to the East of the Rio del Norte were regarded as usurpations. So much for the western limits."

Melish also provided a more specific description of the Rio Grande as the boundary of Louisana:[5, p32] "At the Rio Puerco [Pecos River], the Rio del Norte again becomes the south-west boundary of Louisiana. Below this it runs an east course of between 50 and 60 miles, when it receives a considerable stream from the north [Devils], which is not named on the maps; and hence, without receiving material augmentation, it holds a course nearly south-east, about 400 miles, to the Gulf of Mexico."

Brantz Mayer explained the role of French ownership[6] created by the secret treaty of San Ildefonso in which the King of Spain retroceded Louisiana to the French Republic. The result was described in relation to the Louisiana Purchase: "In 1803, Bonaparte, the first consul of the French republic, ceded Louisiana to the United States, as fully, and in the same manner, as it had been retroceded to France by Spain, under the treaty of San Ildefonso; and, by virtue of this grant, Messrs. Madison, Monroe, Adams, Clay, Van Buren, Jackson, and Polk, contended that the original limit of the new state had been the Rio Grande."

The western limits of Texas by American Presidents continued to be the Rio Grande until the 1819 Adams-Onis (Transcontinental) Treaty that established the boundary between Louisiana and Spanish possessions at the Sabine River and northward. However, despite the treaty not being fully ratified by the King of Spain until February, 1821, settlers from the United States had already moved into Texas based on their Spanish grants from Stephen F. Austin. In addition, the final boundary as described in the treaty was never surveyed or confirmed by either Spain or the United States.

Despite the treaty establishing the boundary between New Spain and the United States, the acquisition of Texas was a major goal of several Presidents, especially Andrew Jackson. After the return of Poinsett from Mexico, he sent a new Consul, Anthony Butler, to Mexico City in 1829[7] despite his knowing that his new appointee was in debt to several individuals and lived in Texas, not Mississippi, as Jackson claimed in his appointment. Butler had only one direct order and responsibility from President Jackson, that is, to purchase Texas from Mexico for no more than five million dollars, but this had an immediate effect on Mexico in the process. The reaction by the Mexican Congress was to pass a new law in 1830 outlawing the migration of Americans to Texas.

Butler's behavior and activities as Jackson's representative in Mexico proved to be disastrous. Despite his lavish living style and marrying a Mexican woman (without divorcing his first wife), he repeatedly created problems between Mexican and American governments. His letters (under the alias, O.P.Q.) in 1834 to Colonel Almonte were directly responsible for the initiation of several actions in Texas. His first letter accused Colonel Almonte of being a "spy" seeking the safest location to attack Texas. His second letter informed Almonte that a group of citizens in Texas were planning an uprising against Mexico. Upon his return from scouting Texas, Almonte's report must have been the reason that General Santa Anna took the first steps to invade Texas. So, President Jackson's choice of a representative set in motion a series of military conflicts that would end with the Treaty of Guadalupe Hidalgo after the loss of thousands of both Mexican and American lives.

Mexican Governance of Texas

What started as a trickle of three hundred families soon became a flood of immigrants from the United States into Texas. Even after Mexico won its independence from Spain on August 23, 1821, only a few months after the Adams-Onis Treaty had finally been signed, the Mexican government supported the settlement of Texas by immigrants from the United States. In time the migration of Americans into Texas created major problems for the Mexican government, but its initial policy was to encourage their settlement in Texas. Considering the massive amount of Spanish territory that Mexico claimed as its own after becoming an independent republic, settling a part of Mexico that had been controlled by hostile Indians for decades was a reasonable plan. Subsequent events showed that Mexico was no better at dealing with Anglo-Americans than with the indigenous tribes spread from Texas westward to California.

Immediately following Mexican independence, Mexico supported the migration of Americans into Texas by giving large land grants (4,428 acres) for a nominal amount of cash ($30). The benefits from attracting new settlers for Mexico were primarily economic but the new Texans were also expected to assist in fighting the almost endless battles with the indigenous Indian tribes, especially the Comanches. The result was that by 1830 the Anglo-Texans outnumbered the Hispano-Texans by more than two to one, a ratio which had increased to ten to one by 1836 when at least 35,000 Anglos were settled in the state.[3, p 659-660] Despite being outlawed by the Mexican government from 1830 to 1833, American migration of into Texas continued.

Ultimately, the conflicts between the Texas migrants and the Mexican government were the result of similar problems that had faced the American colonists. As noted by Fehrenbach:[8] "Both Texas and the colonies were remote from the central authority. Both during their early years were ignored by a government concerned with other matters. Both regions were permitted to exercise local self-government, defend themselves, and build social institutions on their own. Both grew increasingly prosperous. Trouble came in each case only when the central government began to insist upon taxation and collection of customs. Fights with custom officers and the quartering of troops at colonial expense aggravated the situation. The determination to enforce complete obedience, and the dispatch of an army, in 1775 and 1835, brought the colonials flocking to arms."

During this period, changes developed in the government in Mexico finally leading to the declaration of the "Plan of Toluca" that was favored by President Santa Anna.[9] The plan destroyed the "Federative System" and vested the power in a Central Government. State legislatures were abolished and states were changed to Departments under the control of military leaders responsible only to the national authorities. The revolt in Texas had reached the point where a decisive blow had to be struck against the colony. "Accordingly, as soon as Santa Anna had assured himself of the establishment of Centralism, he departed with the flower of his troops to reconquer Texas."

Santa Anna's initial step was to send the army of his brother-in-law, General Cos, to establish Saltillo as the capitol of Coahuila, a "liberal" state, instead of its current capitol, Monclova. Then, after moving his army to the Rio Grande, Cos was ordered to occupy and reinforce the Alamo, a long-abandoned presidio, in San Antonio to oppose the forces of the Texian army. The consequences were disastrous for everyone involved.

Revolution Against Mexico by Republic of Texas

In August 1835, one of those migrating Anglo-Americans, Samuel Augustus (Sam) Maverick, arrived at the port of Velasco with the primary goal of starting a land business in the rapidly growing state.[10] After traveling to San Antonio where he lodged with John W. Smith, Maverick purchased his first land near the city, but his land business ended when General Cos, who had moved his army from Mexico up to the Alamo, put both Maverick and Smith under house arrest. While Cos fortified the Alamo and the plazas, the Texian army located nearby gradually added both men and artillery.

On October 24th, 1835, the Texians began their siege of the Alamo and the army of General Cos but despite continuous arterial barrages nothing was achieved by either the Texians or the Mexicans. Without explanation, General Cos released Maverick and Smith from house arrest, after which they joined the Texian army composed primarily of volunteers with few Texas residents. Smith and Maverick were able to convince the Texians that San Antonio could be captured, so early on the morning of December 5th, an attack upon the city began with the Texian army advancing upon the city in two columns, one led by Johnson with Smith as its scout and the other led by Milam with Maverick as its scout. By fierce house-to-house fighting, the Texians surrounded the Alamo, forcing General Cos to surrender on December 10th.

After General Cos and his men were allowed to leave San Antonio under an agreement never to fight in Texas again, Maverick joined the Alamo garrison of just over a hundred men. When the Independence Convention at Washington-on-the-Brazos was announced for March 1st, Sam Maverick was elected to represent the Alamo garrison. However, the situation for the Texians had changed dramatically because General Santa Anna, after forcing General Cos to re-join the army, crossed the Rio Grande on February 19th. By the 22nd, the rapidly growing Mexican army laid siege to the Alamo and had almost completely surrounded the former presidio by the 28th. On March 2nd, William Travis, commander of the Alamo garrison, sent Sam Maverick to the Independence Convention to seek help for the Alamo defenders.

With John Smith, who had also been sent to ask for help at the Alamo, Maverick arrived at the Independence Convention on Saturday, March

5th, and was seated the following day. Tragically, General Santa Anna and the Mexican army began a successful assault upon the Alamo early that morning and by afternoon, the Alamo had been overrun and its defenders (187) executed. On March 7th, Maverick signed the Texas Declaration of Independence and stayed at the convention to help write the Republic's constitution.

While the constitution was being written, Santa Anna marched eastward, laying waste to the settlements, burning everything in his path. Sam Houston's army of Texians and volunteers retreated before Santa Anna's army until they reached the San Jacinto River bayou country. Then, on April 21st, after cutting off their escape route, Sam Houston and the Texians attacked the Mexican army. With no Mexican guards posted, the Texian army easily reached their barricades and in a very short and intense battle killed half of the Mexican troops, capturing the other half, many of whom were wounded. Although Santa Anna initially escaped, he and General Cos were captured the following day (April 22nd) and brought to General Sam Houston.

After several days of negotiation between Houston and Santa Anna, two agreements, one public and one private, were reached with General Santa Anna on May 14, 1836 at Velasco, Texas.[8] The public Treaty of Velasco included the following major concessions by Santa Anna: 1) Santa Anna swore personally never to take arms against Texas; 2) All hostilities between two nations would cease immediately; 3) The Mexican Army would withdraw below the Rio Grande; 4) All American prisoners still held would be released; 5) The treaty would govern General Filisola, the new Mexican Army commander; and 6) Santa Anna would be shipped to Vera Cruz as soon as possible.

In the private treaty, Santa Anna personally pledged to work within Mexico to achieve four goals: 1) Diplomatic recognition of Texas; 2) Republic of Texas independence; 3) A treaty of commerce; and 4) Recognition of the Rio Grande as the Texas-Mexico boundary. The Supreme Government of Mexico refused to recognize the Treaty of Velasco since General Santa Anna was in captivity when the treaties were signed. In addition, the Mexican Government insisted that all of Texas was still its property despite the declaration of independence by the Republic of Texas.

Recognition of Texas independence by the United States was not easily achieved despite the support of President Andrew Jackson. However, after Martin Van Buren was chosen as Jackson's successor, recognition was approved by the U.S. House of Representatives before barely passing in the U.S. Senate on March 2, 1837, exactly one year after Texas declared its independence. On March 3, 1837, President Jackson, with less than twenty-four hours remaining in his Presidential term, signed legislation recognizing the Republic of Texas.

Annexation of Texas Republic

Despite powerful opposition because of its status as a "slave state," U.S. President John Tyler managed to defeat its opponents and complete the annexation of Texas. Although President Jackson had been supportive of Texas annexation, his major contributions had been to recognize the Republic of Texas and an unsuccessful attempt to purchase Texas from Mexico. Martin Van Buren who succeeded Jackson opposed the admission of Texas, primarily because it was a Southern slave state so the critical event leading to annexation of Texas was the election of General William H. Harrison as Van Buren's successor with John Tyler as his Vice-President.[11] After Harrison's sudden death only a month after his inauguration, John Tyler came to the White House as the last of the U.S. Presidents who were slave-owning Virginia plantation owners. Following Harrison's burial on April 7, 1842, John Tyler was recognized as the new U.S. President by the Senate and House of Representatives on April 9th. Initially expected to be incapable of dealing with Henry Clay and the Whig Party, Tyler proved to be both a stronger and a much better politician than members of his own party had assumed.

As a strict interpreter of the U.S. Constitution, President Tyler opposed the formation of a national bank despite the Whig Party's support. After a second veto of the national bank, Tyler's Cabinet, inherited from President Harrison, resigned en masse except for Daniel Webster. In retaliation for his vetos, President Tyler was expelled from the Whigs on September 13th at a meeting of the Whig Party, making him the first U.S. President to serve "without a party." Ignoring demands that he resign, Tyler continued his Presidency freed from the restraints of supporting a political party's objectives.

The year 1842 was just as difficult for Tyler with another dispute with Congress over passage of a tariff bill, the first of which he vetoed. At the same time, Daniel Webster was negotiating with Lord Ashburton over a treaty establishing the border between the State of Maine and Quebec. It was during this time that John Tyler twice turned down President Houston's request for annexation of Texas because of his involvement with the other issues.

Despite threats of impeachment, negotiations with England and the death of his wife after years of declining health, Tyler's enemies were at least respectful of his grief, permitting his pursuit of foreign affairs. By December, 1842, and despite his grief, President Tyler had extended the Monroe Doctrine to include the Sandwich Islands, i.e. the Tyler Doctrine, as well as opened trade with China. Even after three major accomplishments in foreign affairs, his success was overshadowed by his losing the mother of his eight children. After a brief attempt to remarry, President Tyler turned his attention to the last of his major goals, i.e., the annexation of Texas.

His efforts to annex Texas began by taking two major steps. First, Tyler opened a public campaign, including travel outside of Washington, to promote both Texas annexation and Manifest Destiny, a goal originally proposed by Thomas Jefferson. Second, he re-organized his Cabinet to including such strong supporters of Texas as Abel Upshur to be Secretary of State and Thomas Gilmer, Secretary of the Navy. Upshur immediately started negotiations with the Republic of Texas. However, Sam Houston was reluctant to pursue annexation publicly because of the lack of protection from attacks by Mexico or England.

That only increased the concerns of President Tyler and other supporters of Texas annexation about delaying the process. Besides being an important trade partner of the United States, the Republic of Texas had also been considering other alternatives, possibly with Sam Houston's support. A commercial relationship with England, especially providing cotton for English mills in competition with the American South, had been under consideration ever since Tyler's first rejections of Houston. Texas could also remain an independent republic, especially if lands west to the Pacific were acquired from Mexico with English help, creating a bicoastal nation to serve as a buffer between the United States and English lands. Finally, although unlikely as long as Santa Anna was the dictator, rejoining the Republic of Mexico was also a possibility, considering the centuries-old relationship between the republics.

In February, 1844, despite the reluctance of Houston, Secretary of

State Upshur reached a verbal agreement with Texas representatives to annex the state. Despite the agreement, Sam Maverick, a Member of the Texas Congress, was extremely concerned about both the lack of President Houston's support for annexation and the integrity of the individuals negotiating an agreement. In particular, Maverick was disturbed by Houston's "hatred of the wesern section" and the possibility that the Texas negotiators would "give away the Rio Grande" despite its importance to the future of Texas.[1]

In Washington, the personal life of President Tyler improved with the return of Julia Gardiner to the Capitol with her family. However, his joy would be short-lived when during a cruise down the Potomac River. On February 28th a new cannon, the Peacemaker, on its third and final firing exploded, injuring and killing many of those on the ship. Tragically, Abel Upshur and Thomas Gilmer, Tyler's most ardent supporters of Texas annexation were killed as was David Gardiner, Julia's father, which required her departure from Washington to deal with family affairs.

Despite the loss of close friends and supporters as well as Julia's departure, President Tyler continued his efforts to annex Texas. Without considering the consequences of his offer, Tyler appointed a former U.S. Vice-President, John C. Calhoun of South Carolina, as his new Secretary of State. Calhoun moved quickly to complete negotiations with the Republic of Texas and probably convinced President Tyler of the need to protect Texas against foreign attacks. Using secret Presidential funds, Tyler funded a naval blockade of the Texas Gulf Coast and moved the U.S. Army of the Southwest to the banks of the Sabine River. His provision of protection led to the signing of a formal treaty annexing Texas with Calhoun signing for the United States while Harrison and Van Zandt signed for Texas.

Appointing Calhoun to be Secretary of State was shown to be a mistake when the U.S. Senate debated ratification of the treaty. The public advocate of a state's right to secede, Calhoun also was a zealot in defense of slavery. In supporting the treaty, he emphasized the benefits of Texas being a new slave state in the Union. The result was that the abolitionists and opponents of Western expansion in the Senate rejected the Texas treaty on June 8, 1844. John Tyler had failed to achieve what he felt would be the defining achievement of his administration. However, Tyler was more successful in improving his personal life. On June 26th, Tyler married Julia Gardiner despite the thirty year difference in their ages. His marriage to

Julia proved to be major factor in the annexation of Texas.

After an abortive attempt to form a new political party, John Tyler officially withdrew from the race for U.S. President in favor of the Democrat, James Polk, on August 20, 1844. By carrying states where Tyler was relatively popular, Polk easily defeated Henry Clay, the Whig Party candidate, for the Presidency. However, President Tyler, in his final address to the "lame-duck" Congress, he emphasized that the annexation of Texas was the "will of the people." Julia Tyler, who had already been active in support of Texas, increased her involvement by having parties at the White House and personally lobbying Members of Congress on Capitol Hill on behalf of Texas.

On January 25, 1845, after weeks of debate, the Tylers' political activities resulted in the House of Representatives passing the Texas annexation bill by a vote of 120 to 98. Approval of the bill proved to be more difficult in the Senate where abolitionists were more powerful, but the introduction of a compromise by Mississippi Senator Walker, soon to be Polk's Secretary of the Treasury, gave the President a choice between negotiating with Mexico over Texas annexation or signing the bill into law. The Senate approved the legislation 27 to 25, although neither Walker nor anyone else believed Tyler would sign the bill.

On March 1, 1845, surrounded by supporters of Texas annexation, including his wife, President John Tyler signed the bill annexing Texas just three days before his term ended. Despite infuriating Senator Walker and creating a huge public uproar, the deed had been done: Texas was free to join the Union despite anyone's objection, including Mexico's.

On March 3, 1845, President Tyler and his young wife celebrated their last night in the White House by having a party to which hundreds of people came. Called upon to make a final speech during the party, President Tyler expressed his pride in annexing Texas:[12, p 126] "The day has come when a man can feel proud to be an American citizen. He can stand on the Northeastern boundary or on the shores of the Rio Grande del Norte and contemplate the extent of our vast and growing Republic, the boundaries of which have been settled and extended by peaceful negotiations."

President Tyler clearly believed that the western border of Texas was the Rio Grande.

Before James Polk assumed the Presidency, two significant events occurred while John Tyler was still President. First, under orders from his government, the Mexican ambassador, Juan N. Almonte, asked for his passport and prepared to return to Mexico City. Second, on his last day in office, March 3rd, Tyler sent orders to Andrew Jackson Donelson, his charge' d'affaires in Texas, to inform Sam Houston, the past President, and Anson Jones, the current President of the Republic of Texas, that the United States had decided to annex Texas to the Union. The following day, James Polk was inaugurated as the eleventh American President. During his inaugural address, Polk confirmed his support for the annexation of Texas as a state. In addition he emphasized that the annexation of Texas was a decision that belonged solely to Texas and the United States, thereby excluding any role for England, France or Mexico in negotiations with the Republic of Texas.[13] In addition, at an early meeting, the Polk Cabinet emphasized to Donelson that Texas should not make any changes in the terms of the agreement passed by the U.S. Congress. To demonstrate his support for Texas annexation, Polk sent one of his most faithful supporters, Archibald Yell, to confirm to Jones and Houston that the United States intended to defend Texas territory all of the way from the Sabine River to the Rio Grande.

Political Unrest in Mexico: 1836–1845

Schlarman[14, p 441] summarized the situation in Mexico during the period after the Texas Revolution under the title, IMMIGRATION:

> "The expansion of the [American] frontier, the westward push, was on. The population of the United States increased at a rapid pace: 4,000,000 in 1790 and 9,600,000 in 1820. This was largely owing to immigration. The Napoleonic wars had rudely disturbed the economic security of western continental Europe, absentee landlordism and famines drove the Irish to the United States and Canada, and the industrial revolution in England was hard on the poor. In fact, European governments encouraged emigration to ease the relief load, although, of course, by no means were all of the immigrants paupers. The pressure of immigration in turn pushed the frontier westward.
> In Mexico the situation was different. When Hidalgo raised the battle cry, "Death to the Spaniards!", immigration from Spain ceased. The anti-immigrant spirit continued to the time of Gomez Farias, who hated the Spaniards. The northern European countries had at no time

sent emigrants to Mexico. Actually the United States profited by the coming of immigrants. Mexico lacked this asset in the hour of need.

The northern province of New Spain (Mexico), that is to say, the vast areas south and north of the Rio Grande, Texas, New Mexico, Arizona, California, had really never been a part of the core of New Spain. Apart from several military presidios and the flourishing Catholic missions among the Indians, the viceroys and the succeeding governments paid little attention to the development of these vast areas.

Thus it came about that a handful of Americans could secure the independence of Texas and set up the Texas Republic after Santa Anna's defeat at San Jacinto in 1836. Texas was admitted to the Union on December 29, 1845, and during those nine intervening years Mexico did not send a single military expedition to recapture Texas."

The political chaos in Mexico between 1836 and 1845 had had disastrous effects. First, its central government had been in continuous political turmoil without a reliable leader for over 20 years. Second, the poorly organized Mexican army was incapable of protecting its citizens from Indian depredations in the northern states much less fight a major war with a foreign army. Third, most of the northern territories, originally explored and settled by Spanish Catholic missionaries, had been vacated when the central government confiscated the Church's lands and expelled the Spanish priests. Fourth, millions of dollars owed to both England and the United States could not be re-paid by Mexico, primarily due to expulsion of the Spaniards who had managed their economy. Finally, the silver mines had been closed down because of relentless Apache and Comanche attacks, eliminating that source of revenue. In summary, the Republic of Mexico in 1845 lacked the financial and military resources required either to defend its northern lands against the hostile tribes residing near the Rio Grande or to start a war with the United States.

The Mexican-American War

By order of President Anson Jones, a special session of the Texas Congress met on July 4, 1845 to consider both annexation and approval of a state constitution. Another proposal, a treaty with Mexico which had been urged by Great Britain despite its not specifying the boundary between Texas and Mexico, was also to be discussed. The first action of the Texas Senate was to reject the treaty with Mexico. Then, annexation to the United States and a new state constitution were discussed and approved by both the House and Senate.

While the Texas Congress was approving its annexation, President Polk ordered the American army to cross over into Texas and U.S. naval forces to patrol its coast. From Fort Jessup, Louisiana, Brigadier General Zachary Taylor moved four thousand U.S. troops into Texas as far as Corpus Christi with orders not to allow any opposing forces east of the Rio Grande. On August 29, 1845, the President specifically ordered Taylor to consider any crossing of Rio Grande by the Mexican Army to be an act of war. If American soldiers were attacked, Taylor was to occupy Matamoros and any other Mexican positions located along the river. On January 13, 1846, Polk ordered General Taylor to move his troops from Corpus Christi to the eastern banks of the Rio Grande.

The assumption among U.S. historians for decades has been that the movement of American soldiers to the Rio Grande in the Nueces Strip was the reason why the war between Mexico and the United States began. However, the former Secretary of the U.S. Legation to Mexico 1841–1842, Brantz Mayer provided a much different explanation in his 1852 book about Mexico:[6, p.336] "The true origin of the Mexican war was not this march of Taylor and his troops to the Rio Grande, through the debatable land. The American and Mexican troops were brought face to face by the act, and *hostilities* were the natural result after the exciting annoyances upon the part of the Mexican government which followed the union of Texas with our confederacy. Besides this, General Paredes, the usurping president, had already declared in Mexico, on the *18th of April,* 1846 in a letter addressed to the commanding officer on the northern frontier, that he supposed him as the head of a valiant army on the theatre of action; and that it was indispensable to commence hostilities, *the Mexicans themselves taking the initiative!*

On April 12, 1846 Mexican General Pedro de Ampudia in Matamoros sent General Taylor a demand that the American forces be moved back east of the Nueces River. Shortly thereafter, General Mariano Arista arrived in Matamoros to assume control of Mexican forces from General Ampudia. On April 25, 1846, two companies of U.S. Army dragoons under a Captain Thornton were on patrol twenty-five miles up the Rio Grande. Then, as had been ordered by President Paredes, the American soldiers were surrounded by several hundred Mexican cavalrymen who had crossed the Rio Grande and attacked the U.S. soldiers. In the battle that followed, eleven American dragoons were killed and twenty-six captured, including Captain Thornton. When he learned of the battle the next day, Taylor said, "Hostilities may now be considered as commenced."

Meanwhile, in Washington, the possibility of war with Mexico had been discussed by Polk's Cabinet on May 5, 1846. Three days later, John Slidell returned home and met with Polk about the situation in Mexico. At 6:00 PM on May 9th, the President received a dispatch from General Taylor stating that hostilities had commenced. After spending Sunday preparing his message, on May 11th, Polk requested a declaration of war by Congress on the basis that "American blood had been shed on American soil."[15, p.8] That same day, the declaration of war with Mexico was passed by the House of Representatives. After several hours of debate on the next day, the Senate overwhelmingly passed the declaration. The following day, May 13th, a Congressional delegation delivered the act declaring war on Mexico to President Polk who signed the bill. The United States had officially declared war with Mexico.

The details of the Mexican-American War have been covered in detail many times over the past century and a half, but nothing will be covered here other than the events related to the end of hostilities. On September 12, 1848, American forces under General Winfield Scott staged its last assault on Mexico City, forcing a Mexican delegation to surrender the city on September 14th, a little over two years and four months after Mexican troops had first crossed the Rio Grande to attack American troops above Matamoros. Realizing that defeat was imminent, President Santa Anna fled north with his remaining troops to Guadalupe Hidalgo. There, on September 18th, he resigned the Presidency and on October 1st, was relieved of his military command, after which Santa Anna once again was expelled from Mexico in disgrace.

Mayer[6, p.427] described the events that followed: "The discomfiture of Paredes, the want of pecuniary resources, the disorganization of the country, the growing strength of the Americans who were pouring into the capital under Patterson, Butler and Marshall, and the utter failure of the arch-intriguer [Santa Anna], all contributed to strengthen the arm of the executive and to authorize both the negotiation of a treaty and the arrangement of an armistice until the governments should ratify the terms of peace. Mr. Nicholas P. Trist, Don Luis G. Cuevas, Don Bernardo Coute, and Don Miguel Atristain, signed the treaty, thus consummated, on the 2nd of February, 1848, at the town of Guadalupe Hidalgo. Its chief terms were 1st, the re-establishment of peace;2nd, the boundary which confirmed the southern line of Texas and gave us New Mexico and Upper California; 3rd, the payment of fifteen millions by the United States, in the consideration of the extension of our boundaries; 4th, the payment by our government of all the claims of its citizens against the Mexican Republic to the extent of three and a quarter millions, so as to discharge Mexico forever from all responsibility; 5th, a compact to restrain the incursions and misconduct of the Indians on the northern frontier."

For citizens of northern Mexico who lived along the disputed border, peace in central Mexico had little or no effect on their lives. After Doniphan's Volunteers secured El Paso del Norte and General Taylor occupied Matamoros, no major battles had been fought on or near the Rio Grande between Matamoros and El Paso del Norte by the time the war ended. The reasons were: 1) the American side had been inhabited by indigenous tribes since Spain's abandonment of its presidios; 2) the people of northern Mexico had little or no loyalty to the central government, primarily because the central governments had never supported them; 3) businessmen in the northern states had continued to trade with Texans as they had since the days of New Spain.

However, enforcement of the 5th chief term, i.e., Article XI in the treaty that was finally ratified by both countries on May 30, 1848, proved to be more difficult and expensive to enforce than the United States appreciated.

Treaty of Guadalupe Hidalgo

Peace Treaty and Its Final Approval

The first version of the Treaty of Guadalupe Hidalgo between Mexico and the United States included twenty-three separate articles (I - XXIII), covering many subjects, such as withdrawal of American troops, the boundary line between the two countries, citizenship rights, and property claims. Article XII stated the final purchase price of the northern territories which the U.S. Government was acquiring from Mexico. A total of fifteen million dollars was to be paid to Mexico, starting with an immediate payment of three million dollars. An additional twelve million dollars was scheduled to be as annual payments of three million dollars plus interest. The treaty was changed and amended by the Congresses of both Mexico and the United States before it was finally ratified the on May 30, 1848. The final peace treaty between the two adversaries was proclaimed the law of the land by President James Polk on July 4, 1848.[13]

Rio Grande As Texas-Mexico Border

Although the conflicts over the border between Mexico and the Republic of Texas, as well as with the United States, have been mentioned several times, the Treaty of Guadalupe Hidalgo finally established the Rio Grande, from the Gulf of Mexico up to a new line separating New Mexico Territory from Mexico, as the border between Texas and Mexico despite Mexico having opposed that boundary since the Treaty of Velasco. In many ways, the dispute over the Rio Grande was almost ridiculous since no country had ever established secure and stable control over the northern frontier of Mexico.

In reality, the true northern border of Mexico was not even as far north as the original Spanish "line of defense." Most of the original Spanish presidios had been abandoned or lacked adequate support from the central government of Mexico to function. The reality was that the Mexican government did not exist north of El Paso del Norte, except along the Camino Real to northern New Mexico and Santa Fe. The disputed lands between the Nueces River and the Rio Grande, the so-called "Nueces Strip," were under frequent attacks by several tribes, especially the Comanches, who could travel freely across the "Strip" with little or no opposition from either Mexico or Texas. Thus, the Rio Grande as the border between Texas and Mexico was not accepted and agreed upon until the Treaty of Guadalupe Hidalgo. The final border was to be determined by a binational Boundary Commission that would survey and define the legal border between the two countries.

American Obligations Under Article XI of Treaty

Significance of Article XI of Treaty

However, one article of the Treaty, Article XI, added new responsibilities for the U.S. Government which would prove to be unexpectedly expensive.[16] Specifically, the first paragraph of Article XI stated that "a great part of the territories which...for the future within the limits of the United States, is now occupied by "savage tribes," who will hereafter be under the exclusive control of the Government of the United States, and whose incursions within the territory of Mexico would be prejudicial in the extreme; ... It is solemnly agreed that all such incursions shall be forcibly controlled by the Government of the United States, " The United States assumed exclusive responsibility not only over the "savage tribes" in the new territories but also for the prevention of their incursions into Mexico. The President and U.S. Senate, including Texas' own Senator, Sam Houston, accepted an obligation to control the "savage" inhabitants of the new territories despite having almost no knowledge about which tribes were "savage" and where they were crossing the border.

Multiple Obligations Assumed By United States

As noted by Howe,[3] accepting responsibility for controlling the tribes living north of the new border was a major concession by Nicholas Trist in reaching the final peace treaty with Mexico and the United States Government was forced to take several immediate steps. The route for an east-west wagon road from San Antonio to both Chihuahua and El Paso had to be located, then a road built. Construction of forts at critical locations on the road would be required for the protection of travelers through the new lands. And, to meet the most difficult responsibility, the Rio Grande crossings along the border, where Indians entered Mexico to attack its pueblos and people, had to be found. Exploration of the new United States-Mexico border, which was in the midst of lands occupied by an unknown numbers of hostile Indians, was an immediate requirement if Indian depredations in Mexico were to be stopped.

Americans Ability to Enforce Article XI

Over a century and a half later, the complexities of America's new responsibilities are difficult to appreciate. Early Spanish explorers since Cabeza de Vaca first walked across the Southwest had traveled across the newly acquired lands, but Americans knew very little about the region. Even though all lands east of the Rio Grande had been claimed by the Republic of Texas as its territory since 1836, only relatively small areas had been controlled by either Texas or Mexico. Indigenous Indian tribes, among which were the Comanche, Apache, Navajo, and Kiowa tribes, controlled the territories on both sides of the Rio Grande. The situation was clearly described by Hart when he wrote in that "The United States found it had assumed an almost unwelcome burden when it took over the Southwest. It promised protection and peace to the settlers—and to Mexico—and it had not the wherewithal to do the job."[17]

The "Apacheria" and the "Comancheria"

After winning its independence from Spain, the Republic of Mexico claimed the lands that had originally been Spanish territory. However, the basis for ownership of the lands Mexico sold to the United States government was tenuous at best for a simple reason: the borderlands along the Rio Grande at the time of the Treaty of Guadalupe Hidalgo were occupied and controlled by two major native tribes, the Apaches (the *"Apacheria"*) and the Comanches (the *"Comancheria"*). Numerous other native tribes lived in the territories that the United States purchased, although their survival as well as those of the Hispanic inhabitants were dependent in many ways on the whims and wishes of the two dominant tribes.

After the Northern Line of Defense, a series of presidios stretching from the Gulf of California to the mouth of the Guadaupe River in Texas, had been established by a Royal Edict in 1773, the activities of the Apaches, especially the Lipan Apaches, had increased, expanding the *Apacheria* in northern Mexico. To deal with the problem, the Spanish King created the Interior Provinces, a military district on the northern frontier under a Commandant General. After meetings in Texas and Coahuila, a Council of War was held by the Commandant in Chihuahua June 9-15, 1778 to develop a plan to control the growing *Apacheria*.[18, p. 23-25] The Council found that separating the presidios from the Spanish settlements had weakened the defenses on the northern. The Apaches were de-populating the once fertile provinces. Even worse, no one knew how many Apaches were living in the Apacheria from which they attacked the Spanish provinces.

The solution, "a new defense policy for the northern frontier," was to form an alliance with the northern tribes, in effect, the Comanches, the ferocious enemies of the Lipans, to defeat the *Apacheria* as the Marquis de Rubi had suggested. The results of the new policy were disastrous because as the Apaches were almost annihilated by the alliance, the Comanches increased their activities in what had been the Apacheria. Initially, limited to the High Plains and Edwards Plateau in Texas, the Comanches expanded their incursions into northern and central Mexico, replacing the *Apacheria* with the *Comancheria*. With Mexico winning its independence from Spain and the birth of the Republic of Texas, the *Comancheria* was pushed to the west and south, even deeper into Mexico.

To describe the extent of control by the Apache and Comanche raiders, Weber[19] quoted a statement by the Chihuahuan legislature: we travel the roads... at their whim; we cultivate the land where they wish and in the amount they wish; we use sparingly thing they have left us until the moment it strikes their appetite to take them for themselves. Hamalainen[21] further described the conditions in northern Mexico at the time of the Treaty of Guadalupe Hidalgo: "Mexico City's failure to restrain Comanches had also thwarted its hopes to reconquer Texas. During the years following the Texas revolt, Comanches extended their stock-and-slave raiding operations deep into northern Mexico, wreaking havoc in seven departments. Not only did the recapture of Texas become impossible, but the entire northern part of the nation began to slip out of Mexico City's grip. Citizens across all the north were perturbed by the federal government's inability — and apparent unwillingness — to curb Comanche raids, and they grew increasingly alienated from Mexico City and its nation-building project. The linkages between American and Comanche expansions climaxed in the Mexican-American War. When the U.S. Army marched south of the Rio Grande in 1846, Comanches had already turned vast segments of Mexico's heart land into an economically underdeveloped, politically fragmented, and psychologically shattered world that was ripe for conquest by Americans, who, in a sense, came to occupy what was a vanquished hinterland of Greater

Comancheria. In northern Mexico, U.S. imperialism was the direct heir to Comanche imperialism."

The extent to which the Comanches had expanded their activities in northern Mexico was noted by Sam Maverick in 1842.[1] The following entry in his journal about the march from Texas down to Perote Prison east of Mexico City after being captured by General Woll describes an earlier attack (1839) by the Comanches in Mexico. This entry was written after several earlier entries in his journal had mentioned evidence of Indian depredations along their route to central Mexico.

> *"Nov. 11th - Fine Hall and Mazon of Salado. Wagon load of wool. The Comanches (1839) did worse here than at San Salvador, where they put the women in a house and burned them. This morning pass a well where is the corner of three or four states, viz: [Coahuila, Nuevo Leon, Zacatecas, San Luis Potosi]."*

El Salado is about 80 miles south of Saltillo in the state of San Luis Potosi, just across the border from the state of Zacatecas. Saltillo, the capital of Coahuila, is located in the southern region of the state 300 miles due south of the Texas-Mexico border at Lozier Canyon, the site of a major Indian trail entering Mexico. Maverick's journal entry also emphasizes how far the Comanche would ride to attack Mexican villages and ranches as well as how cruel and barbaric their attacks could be.

The replacement of the presidio-mission system by Spain with a line of defense of presidios stretching across northern Mexico had been a total failure. Forming an alliance with the Comanches had intensified the raids by Comanches and Apaches in Mexico to the point where the territories of northern Mexico had become a *despoblado* with few settlers except in those communities that survived by providing supplies for the "hostile" tribes for raids into Mexico. The activities of those tribes had created a *terra incognita* in the territories that the United States eventually bought from Mexico as part of the peace treaty.

The Treaty of Guadalupe Hidalgo agreed upon by the neighboring republics produced a dramatic change in the control of the American Southwest, as noted by Hamalainen:[20, p 192] "The Treaty of Guadalupe Hidalgo ushered in a new order in the Southwest. The United States secured its hold on Texas and absorbed New Mexico, extending its possessions from the

Nueces River to the Rio Grande. In Article Eleven of the treaty, the United States agreed to police the border to prevent Indian raiders from crossing the Rio Grande into Mexico. For the Comanches, this was unfathomable: their home territory had fallen squarely within the borders of a vastly more powerful nation that meant to box them in and tie them down. That pressure, meted out by the U.S. military, federal agents, and soldier-settlers, began immediately after the Mexican-American War and increased steadily until the Civil War and its aftermath brought a brief respite."

2
OBJECTIVES AND MEMBERS OF THE 1848 PIONEER EXPEDITION

> "One cannot understand history until one has stood in the place and surveyed the land. See the land as they saw it; listen to the story the land tells. Armchair research only goes so far."
> — Louis F. Aulbach[21]

Objectives of the 1848 Chihuahua-El Paso Pioneer Expedition

On July 4, 1848, President James Polk proclaimed that the Treaty of Guadalupe Hidalgo between Mexico and the United States was the "law of the land," officially establishing the Rio Grande as the border between Mexico and Texas.[13] The U.S. Government was immediately faced with innumerable problems since the 1848 treaty had added more lands to the continental United States than it had acquired with the Louisiana Purchase in 1803. In addition, the new western territories were markedly different in many ways compared to those added by the 1803 Louisiana Purchase with its Missouri-Mississippi river system and abundant water supply. Although the Rio Grande is the largest river system flowing through the new American territories, the Rio Grande and its tributaries are not suitable for river travel since most of the new lands surrounding the river are desert or mountainous with water available only at scattered "oases." In addition, east-west travel through the newly-acquired lands between Texas and California was almost impossible since no east-west road along or near the border had ever been built. Besides that, an east-west route would have to cross lands occupied by indigenous tribes, most of whom were hostile toward any group of travelers that entered their lands. Soon to create even worse problems, the demand for such a road "exploded" with the discovery of gold in California, rapidly increasing immigration through Texas to California.

Those problems were complicated the fact that few Americans, including those who had lived in the Republic of Texas, knew where the border, as defined by the Rio Grande between Texas and Mexico, was located. Despite being ignorant about what was in the region west of the Texas settlements, the State of Texas claimed all lands east of the Rio Grande, including most of New Mexico, as its property, just as the Republic of Texas had. Except for members of the indigenous tribes who had crossed the border on raids in Mexico for decades, few Texas inhabitants, if any, knew where a route for a road west to Presidio del Norte and El Paso del Norte in Chihuahua could be built.

A group of San Antonio businessmen realized the potential financial rewards of having an east-west road to Chihuahua, so they quickly provided support for an expedition to locate a route for a wagon road from San Antonio to Chihuahua and El Paso, the initial objective of the 1848 Pioneer expedition. A year-round wagon road to Chihuahua that would bring silver and copper from the mines in Mexico to San Antonio and the Texas Gulf Coast by a shorter route than any existing trade route and had the potential to produce huge economic benefits for San Antonio. Unfortunately, the businessmen had no way to know that raids by the Apaches and Comanches had forced closure of the Chihuahua silver mines and almost all ranches, except for very large, fortress-like haciendas. Most workers who had been living in smaller Mexican pueblos and ranches had been captured for ransom or enslavement. Only those who had abandoned the northern frontier before Indian depredations destroyed what they had built managed to survive.

The benefits of such an expedition were so obvious that the San Antonio businessmen provided the initial funding for an expedition and recruited Colonel John (Jack) Hays, the famous Texas Ranger and hero of the war with Mexico, to lead the exploration of the lands west of the city as far as Presidio del Norte and El Paso del Norte. However, the San Antonio group was not the only group interested in a finding a defensible route west from San Antonio to El Paso del Norte, New Mexico and California. Both the State of Texas and the United States Government had interests which led to their support of the 1848 Hays exploration in its search for a route to El Paso. So, the second objective was the immediate exploration of the lands along new border between Texas and Mexico, a step critical to travel through and settlement in both the State of Texas and the southwestern United States. Apparently, through negotiations with the Federal Government, Jack Hays was to be rewarded with an appointment as Indian Agent for the Gila tribe in Arizona

However, a wagon road to El Paso and California was especially important to the U.S. Government because, under Article XI of the Treaty of Guadalupe Hidalgo, the United States had agreed to assume responsibility for preventing raids into Mexico by "the hostile savages" from the vast new lands it had just acquired from Mexico. The American government knew almost nothing about the region, including how many "hostile savage" tribes lived along or north of the new boundary between Mexico and the United States. Even worse, the map (Disturnell's) used to negotiate the Treaty of Guadalupe Hidalgo with Mexico was so inaccurate that the final border between Mexico and the U.S.A. was not established until after a binational Boundary Commission surveyed the new border from the Pacific to the Gulf of Mexico.

Related to finding the route for a wagon road was a third objective that has received little attention in the past, that is, locating crossings along the Rio Grande where tribes from north of the border entered Mexico on raids and, in effect, controlled the northern frontier of Mexico. U.S. Army wagon trains had to have a road across western Texas to provide supplies for forts where U.S. Army troops would be garrisoned to enforce the treaty obligations to control the indigenous tribes in the new territory. That is why Sam Maverick found it so important to include multiple entries in his journal about Indian trails and where they crossed the Rio Grande. With the U.S. government's obligation to prevent Indian incursions across the border, locating the trails by which the different tribes crossed over into Mexico was critical information if the U.S. Army were to be successful in preventing future incursions as required by Article XI of the treaty. The inclusion of Delaware Indians as trackers in the 1848 Expedition supports the importance of their ability to identify which "hostile savages" had been using the trails for raids into Mexico.

Thus, to meet all of its objectives during a single exploration along the new Texas-Mexico border up the Rio Grande to El Paso del Norte, the Chihuahua-El Paso Pioneer Expedition of 1848 had to: 1) discover a feasible route on the American side of the Rio Grande where a wagon road could be built from San Antonio to El Paso del Norte and Chihuahua; 2) locate the new Texas-Mexico border, at least upriver from today's Del Rio (San Felipe Springs) to El Paso del Norte; and 3) find and identify, if possible, the river crossings where "hostile" tribes entered Mexico for raids on its people, property, and especially their animals. Successful completion of even one objective while exploring the vast, uninhabited *terra incognita* along the Rio Grande would require all of the skills of the veteran Texas frontiersmen who volunteered to join the Expedition.

Major Groups Involved

San Antonio Volunteers

The Chihuahua-El Paso Pioneer Expedition was composed of three major groups.[26] The first group included fifteen members from the San Antonio community selected by Colonel Hays, although some members of the group may have been San Antonio businessmen who initially proposed and funded the 1848 expedition. Hays inclusion of Maverick and Howard in the expedition confirmed his confidence in their knowledge and experiences along the western Texas frontier, especially as surveyors.

Texas Rangers (Mounted Volunteers)

Although the Castell contingent in the Pioneer Expedition's forces was said to have been composed of Texas Rangers, they were actually veterans of the Mexican-American War. As members of the First Regiment, Texas Mounted Volunteers under Colonel John C. Hays, who had fought valiantly from the first days near Matamoros until the war ended in Mexico City on September 14, 1847. The Mounted Volunteers were such ferocious, and often merciless fighters, that the Mexicans called them "Los Diablos Tejanos" with more than a little justification. In fact, after the American victory, they raised so much hell and caused so much trouble with both the Mexican people and the regular U.S. Army soldiers that the Army commanders shipped them back to Texas in April, 1847.

Based on the timing of their mustering out and re-organization, the Mounted Volunteers were converted from fighting Mexican soldiers to defending the Texas frontier.[22] For example, Company "D" under Captain Samuel Highsmith was mustered out on May 14, 1848 and reorganized as Captain Samuel Highsmith's Company on May 15, 1848 as part of Lieutenant Colonel. P. Hansbrough Bell's Regiment, Texas Mounted Volunteers. That event occurred between the signing of the Treaty of Guadalupe Hidalgo and its ratification by both the U.S. and Mexican Congresses, the final step required before Mexico's occupation by American troops would officially end. The term of Highsmith's company was from May 15 to December 26, 1848, after which they were to be mustered out at San Antonio.

Captain Highsmith's Company was assigned to the frontier at Camp Llano on the Llano River near Castell, Texas, the only surviving German town of four built along the Llano. Originally, the company included four officers, nine non-commissioned officers, and eighty-five privates, including the Delaware Indian, John Conner. From this company, thirty-five members, including Samuel Highsmith, joined the Chihuahua-El Paso Pioneer Expedition under their former leader, Jack Hays. During the Pioneer Expedition they were well prepared to defend the expedition just as they had in Mexico as "Los Diablos Tejanos."

Delaware Indians

The third group, ten Delaware Indians led by John Conner, another veteran of the Mexican War, lived at or near the Castell camp and the reason for their inclusion has been described by Parker: "Wherever they are found, they preserve the same character for truth, honesty, and intelligence, and are ever ready, at a moment's warning, to take service, as hunters, guides, or interpreters, and travel off hundreds of miles from home. They serve entirely in these capacities, and are universally known and esteemed by travelers in our wild territories, in fact, it is almost impossible to get any other Indians to perform these duties; they are either too selfish, too lazy, or too ignorant, and when applied for, always make the same reply, 'Delaware he do dat, may be so you get him.'"[25]

Parker also made specific comments about the Delawares' abilities as trackers in a footnote: "It was surprising how readily and with what accuracy in detail our Delawares would designate the tribe, the number and disposition of the Indians, who had occupied the deserted camps we met with during our whole trip, and as we met with some of the same parties afterwards, their sagacity in this respect was fully established." If the 1848 Pioneer Expedition were to locate trails where "hostile savages" were invading Mexico, the scouting and tracking skills of the Delawares added critically required expertise to the expedition.

Leaders of the Expedition

Colonel John (Jack) Hays

Although the names of the San Antonio businessmen who initiated and provided funding for the expedition to Chihuahua and El Paso remain unknown, the person chosen to lead the Expedition was the Texas Ranger and Mexican-American War hero, Colonel John Coffee (Jack) Hays. A native of Wilson County, Tennessee, Hays first joined the Texan Army after the Battle of San Jacinto at nineteen years of age before moving to San Antonio as a deputy surveyor. During Indian fights while out on surveying parties, Hays demonstrated such exceptional military and leadership skills that he was asked to organize and command San Antonio's voluntary "Minutemen" of which Sam Maverick was a member. Because of his success in fighting Indians and Mexican bandits along Texas' western frontier, Hays had been commissioned as the first Captain of the Texas Rangers by the Texas Congress in 1840.

When volunteers for the U.S. Army were being recruited to fight in the Mexican-American War, Jack Hays initially joined Company B of First Regiment, Texas Mounted Riflemen as a private, but was quickly promoted to Colonel and commander of the Texas Mounted Volunteers.[22] As the Volunteers leader in Mexico, Hays and the Texans played important roles while serving as scouts and guerrillas for the Army. Despite their undisciplined behavior, the Texans made significant contributions to several American victories. Hays many successes, both as the first Colonel of the Texas Rangers and as leader of the Texas Mounted Volunteers, during the Mexican war were the major reasons why Jack Hays was chosen to lead the expedition into the *terra incognita* between San Antonio and Chihuahua/El Paso del Norte.

Samuel Augustus Maverick (SAM)

Despite his reluctance to join the San Antonio members of the expedition, Samuel Augustus Maverick finally joined the Expedition after Jack Hays convinced his wife, Mary Maverick, that SAM's deteriorating health would improve only with a return to the western frontier.

A native of Pendleton, South Carolina, Maverick had developed a well-deserved reputation as a Texas leader during the Republic's early years, which added credibility, financial strength and frontier skills to the Expedition's efforts. The entries recorded in SAM's daily journal as the Pioneer Expedition explored the lands in western Texas are the only written record of the exploration.[1] Maverick's expertise as a combination surveyor/attorney may have been the reason for Hays persistence in having Maverick join the Expedition, but a story from Mary Maverick's memoirs provides a more personal reason for SAM's joining the expedition.[23]

"The poor child, with crimson cheek and shining eyes, sometimes raved wildly—once she screamed out in agonizing manner: "Oh, Sam," she thought she saw Indians about to kill Sam. When she took her medicine, (the first in her life), she would say, "Mamma, will you tell papa that I took my medicine?" Once she said, "Mamma, if I die _____", but I couldn't bear it—I stopped her before she could speak another word. Ah, how often have I regretted my action, and fondly longed to know what the dear angel would have said. Her father was still out on his surveying expedition on the Las Moras, and we had no means of communicating with him. On May 8th, the poor child breathed her last at two a.m., Tuesday, May 9th, 1848. Even now, in 1880, after 32 years, I cannot dwell on that terrible bereavement. the child was the perfection of sweetness and beauty and possessed such a glad and joyous disposition that her very presence was a flood of sunshine."

"Friday, May 26th, Mr. Maverick returned. Eleven miles west of town, he met an acquaintance who told him of Agatha's death! He went to the grave and threw himself down upon it, and remained there until dark. No one but God could tell the depth of his anguish. He was crushed and broken when he came home. He said he was striving "not to murmur at the will of God." He said we should humble ourselves in sack cloth and ashes—and he never removed that sack cloth in spirit whilst he lived—was ever after a changed man.

In August Colonel Hays was ordered to open a shorter and better trading route through the wilds to Chihuahua, Mexico. Colonel Hays asked me to persuade Mr. Maverick to go with the expedition. I answered: "Oh no, he is not well enough for such a hard trip." Then Hays replied, "Don't you see Mr. Maverick is dying by inches? Every one remarks how gray he has grown, how bent and feeble he looks, and this will be the very thing for him—he always thrives on hardships, and his mind must be distracted from his grief."

I recognized the truth and force of this reasoning and that Hays loved him dearly and I set to work to persuade him to go. My husband was quite reasonable, and quickly saw that the trip had become a necessity for him."

Despite the depth of his personal grief, Samuel Maverick was uniquely qualified to keep the only daily journal about the 1848 Expedition's exploration since, besides his earlier journals about travels in early-day Texas, Maverick had been involved in many early Texas frontier activities. Several of those activities have already been described, i.e., serving as a scout for the Texian Army's capture of the Alamo, signing the Declaration of Independence of the Republic of Texas at Washington-on-the-Brazos as a representative of the Alamo defenders, helping write the Constitution of the Republic of Texas, fighting Indian depredations as a member of Colonel Jack Hays' "Minutemen," and serving as San Antonio's representative in the Republic of Texas Congress that approved annexation.

Sam Maverick also had two unique qualifications as an important member of the Expedition. First, besides being an attorney, he was a surveyor who could accurately record the expeditions travels along the border just as he had as a captive on the way to Perote Prison in Mexico. Second, he had also acquired Las Moras Springs, from which the group would ride west. On his trip to the springs, his surveying party had traveled down Las Moras Creek to the Rio Grande, then up the river to the Devils River before returning to Las Moras. Thus, he knew more about the lands west of San Antonio on their proposed route, at least up to the Devils River, than any other member of the expedition.

Richard A. (Dick) Howard

Another member of the San Antonio group who brought significant frontier experience to the exploration was Richard A. (Dick) Howard, although his major contributions came after the 1848 Expedition. Originally a cadet at the U.S. Military Academy at West Point, NY, from which most of the U.S. Army's frontier officers had graduated, Howard's failure to pass a one class his senior year kept him from graduating with the 1845 class. However, his association with Lieutenants William Whiting and William Smith, his 1845 classmates at West Point, added to his role in exploration of western Texas.

Just as Jack Hays had, Howard joined Company B of the Texas Mounted Riflemen in 1846, but was quickly promoted to Second Lieutenant during the war with Mexico.[22] After the Texas volunteers returned home, Howard worked as a surveyor until his military and frontier experience led to his joining the 1848 Expedition. Howard's subsequent contributions during the 1849 Reconnaissance to El Paso led by Lieutenant Whiting and Smith proved to be even more critical to his former classmates' reconnaissance to El Paso. His knowledge of the region's dangers and terrain, gained while a member of the 1848 Pioneer Expedition, was critical to the survival and success of the Second Exploration. As a participant in the first explorations of the border from the Devils River to El Paso, Howard and two other members of Whiting-Smith's reconnaissance were the first American men to have traveled the entire length of the Rio Grande from Del Rio up to New Mexico.

Dick Howard continued his activities in western Texas by serving as a guide for the Johnston-Van Horne expedition after his return with the Whiting and Smith expedition. As the scout who had discovered the Devils' River section of what became the "Lower Road," Howard served as the guide for Colonel Johnston and Lieutenant Smith of the U.S. Army Engineers as they built the new wagon road from San Antonio to El Paso during his third trip through far West Texas. His name can still be found on a broad canyon, Howard Draw, west of Ozona, Texas, evidence of his role in opening up far West Texas to travelers.

Captain Samuel Highsmith

Captain Samuel Highsmith, leader the Texas Ranger camp at Castell, Texas, was also a veteran of many Indian fights as well as battles with Mexican troops during the Mexican-American War. It was Captain Highsmith who told Mary Maverick that her husband, Sam Maverick, had been captured and was being taken back to Mexico by General Woll's Mexican Army in

San Antonio. As it was for many other Texans, Woll's attack on San Antonio was the renewal of hostilities between Mexico and the Republic of Texas.

Before Highsmith established a ranger camp at Castell, he had commanded Company D of the First Regiment, Texas Mounted Volunteers, under Colonel Jack Hays in Mexico. When Company D was mustered out, it was re-organized as Captain Highsmith's Company at Camp Llano, the westernmost of the 1848 Ranger camps.[24] While stationed there, Highsmith was ordered to join the Pioneer Expedition as the leader of a contingent of thirty-five veteran Mounted Volunteers under his old commander, Jack Hays. His experiences in Mexico and on the Texas frontier made his well qualified to lead the rangers.

John Conner

Of the principal leaders, John Conner, leader of the Delaware Indians contingent, may have received the least credit for his contributions. Listed as a private in Captain Samuel Highsmith's company on the LLano River, Conner was a veteran of the Mexican-American War and one of the most gifted Indian scouts working for the United States Army and Texas Rangers. His skill at identifying the tribe and the number of their animals was particularly important on an expedition into a region controlled by the Comanches and Apaches.

Since finding Indian trails and crossings along the Rio Grande was an objective, Conner's role in the exploration was an important one. Parker described Conner's exceptional skills as a tracker as follows:[25] "In passing down the bed of the stream, in the afternoon, we came upon an Indian trail, when Conner displayed the extraordinary powers he possessed of designating by the mere tracks in the sand the character of the trail. Riding along with his eyes bent upon the sand, he soon stopped, and said, 'Witchita trail, may be so, eight animal, two horse, one pony, three mule, horse shod all round, pony too; shoes on pony old; one mule shod all round, others shod before; trail five days old.'

How he could be so accurate, he knows best, with nothing but some tracks in the sand, partly blown over by the wind, to guide him; but suffice it to say he was correct, which we ascertained two months afterwards; the horses and mules having been stolen from the neighborhood of Fort Belknap, and a detachment of dragoons having been sent out after the marauders.

Such is force of habit, and most invaluable is this power in a country where stock is liable at any hour to be stolen."

The 1848 Pioneer Expedition,[1] composed of "50 armed men and 10 Delaware Indians," that rode up the Llano River was the first American exploration of the lands west of the Devil's River. Considering the years they spent fighting on the Texas frontier and in the Mexican War, the Pioneer Expedition's members were a formidable fighting force, fully capable of defending the exploration from attacks by either indigenous tribes or Mexican bandits. In August, 1848, that combination of skills and experience was essential to an exploration west of San Antonio since no east-west wagon road had ever been built between San Antonio and either Presidio del Norte or El Paso del Norte. In fact, neither Spain nor Mexico had built even a trail along what was now the American side of the Rio Grande. Except for the old "presidio road" along the northern line of defense on the Mexican side, the only existing trails in far west Texas had originally been north-south trails used by the indigenous tribes since prehistoric times.

3

Rendezvous at Las Moras Springs / The Edwards Plateau

This section of the book covers the period during which the San Antonio members of the exploration traveled from the city up to Castell on the Llano River. The reason for the ride to the Llano River was to ask for volunteers from Captain Samuel Highsmith's ranging company and for guides from the Delawares who worked with Highsmith's rangers at Camp Llano. From Castell, the plan was to travel south to Las Moras Springs (later the site of Fort Clark) to meet a "mining group" who planned to search for potential mines while the Hays expedition scouted a wagon road route to Chihuahua and El Paso. Taking a route up to Castell, then down to the springs, proved to waste valuable time and resources intended for use on the Expedition's objectives.

The daily entries from Sam Maverick's journal describing the Pioneer Expedition of 1848[1] are shown in italics in the text. Discussion or descriptions of the Expedition's travels or campsite follow in plain text. Daily mileages from SAM's journal are not included, except where critical to the daily entry. but the GPS locations of the campsites will be included in an Appendix. Sub-sections are shown in underlined plain text to separate discussion of the exploration from that which is indirectly related to the Expedition.

San Antonio to Las Moras Springs

El Paso route with Hayes.
(50 Armed men and 10 Delaware Indians)

27th August 1848 set out from San Antonio for Presidio del Norte etc.
1st day to head of Olmos.

This August 27, 1848 entry was Sam Maverick's first into his daily journal which he kept about the 1,303 mile route that the Chihuahua-El Paso Pioneer Expedition of 1848 traveled in its exploration of the new

Texas-Mexico border and the subsequent return home through the TransPecos. Although not specifically stated, the Expedition members probably gathered in downtown San Antonio after which they rode up the road beside the San Antonio River to its headsprings before continuing up the road along Olmos Creek to its head where the creek ends.

Our journey to re-explore the trail of the Pioneer Expedition also began where the original expedition started, in downtown San Antonio, but at Jim Keller's home in the King William District by which the San Antonio River flows. We were fortunate in having modern roads and highways on which to drive initially, but Jack Hays, Sam Maverick and the thirteen other members of the San Antonio contingent took the Fredericksburg road to the Olmos Creek headsprings. The road up to the head of Olmos Creek for their first campsite is now blocked by the Olmos Dam, which was built to prevent the disastrous floods from flowing into downtown San Antonio. Within its basin, Olmos Creek is an intermittent stream which becomes a floodway only after collecting rain falling from higher elevations but the basin is so large that huge amounts of water can flow into the San Antonio River. With more and more impervious cover being added upstream, there is little doubt about the need for constructing a dam on the creek.

However, despite its unquestionable benefits, the Dam is also responsible for the destruction of a major archeological site during its re-construction. Euro-Americans have periodically traversed the basin for only a few centuries, but they are far from being the earliest humans to camp in the Olmos Basin. For almost 10,000 years, dating back to the Paleo-Indians, humans have camped and lived around the group of springs which form the headwaters of the San Antonio River, including at a site under the dam.[28] Apparently the abundance of game with fresh water led the early hunter-gatherers to use the basin as sites for periodic habitation.

In fact, many of the trails over which the Pioneer Expedition traveled were established pathways which Native Americans had used for their periodic migrations or for trading with other tribes for centuries. For example, their first campsite at the head of Olmos Creek was close by the Pavo Real archeological site, which had been found accidentally during the construction of the intersection of Interstate 10 and Loop 1604 north of San Antonio.[27] Artifacts collected at the site confirmed that Paleo-Indians had been using the site for a camp as far back as 8000 B.C. Thus the first road upon which the Pioneer Expedition started its exploration had been in use not just for decades and centuries, but for millennia.

The ancient trail or road up Olmos Creek was just one of many trails established by Native Americans that the Expedition traveled before their return home to San Antonio. All of the regions which the Pioneer Expedition explored had been inhabited for hundreds, if not thousands, of years before Sam Maverick and his fellow explorers entered what was an unexplored region, at least to Euro-Americans. Finding and following those Indians' trails was also one of the reasons for the 1848 Expedition.

2nd day, August 28th: Cibolo creek.

After camping at the last spring on the Olmos, the ride north up the valley to Cibolo Creek to where they camped overnight near present-day Boerne, Texas was relatively easy on the road to Fredericksburg.

3d day, August 29th to Sisty's creek.

From the Cibolo, the road begins its ascent into the Hill Country north of the San Antonio. First, they climbed over a divide and down into the Guadalupe River basin where they crossed the river at a ford, probably where West Sister's Creek flows into the Guadalupe where they camped on the creek. Whether Sisty's, the name SAM used, was a person's name or a nickname for "sister," makes little difference since Sisterdale, Texas, through which West Sister Creek flows, is still located on the old road to Fredericksburg.

4th day, August 30th to Fredericksburg.

From "Sisty's" the San Antonio group climbed up into the Hill Country, crossing Grape Creek near Luchenbach, now famous because of a country song, and continued up to Fredericksburg. Just south of town, they forded the Pedernales River near Baron's Creek along which they rode to Camp Houston, later to be called Fort Martin Scott. The Fort had a very short life (1848–1853) since the U.S. Army moved the soldiers north to the newly built Fort Mason which was a better site for defending against Indian attacks, no longer a problem for Fredericksburg.

Fredericksburg, one of the two primary German settlements founded by the *Mainzer Adelsverein* ("The Mainz Society of Noblemen"), was a major center for German immigrants to Texas.[24] The Society had been formed for the protection of immigrants in Texas, but after a brief period had no role in the emigration of Germans to Texas. The Society ended in bankruptcy, primarily due to their land grant being too far from existing civilization with little arable land in the middle of Comanche territory. However, the lands north of Fredericksburg along to the Llano River had been freed from Comanche attacks due to an agreement which made settlement of the Llano River much safer than in other parts of the region. As part of an agreement, four small German towns were founded but only one, Castell, named for Count von Castell, business manager for the *Adelsverein*, survived. In 1848 the town of Castell was especially important to the Pioneer Expedition since it was located across the Llano River from the westernmost Texas Ranger post under the command of Captain Samuel Highsmith.

Sept. 1st, to Highsmith's camp (Llano).

On August 31st, Hays and the San Antonio contingent left for Castell, most likely by traveling along Baron's Creek which flows through Fredericksburg from the north, to recruit volunteers from the Ranger camp for the Expedition. The last day's ride to Highsmith's camp across from Castell was significant for two reasons. The first was that they had arrived at Highsmith's Ranger camp to ask for volunteers to join the Expedition. The second was one which few members, other than Sam Maverick, knew existed, i.e. their entry into a geologically unique area of Texas, the Llano Uplift. SAM apparently recognized how special the place was since he had already filed a claim for the land around the Enchanted Rock, located east of Castell. By gaining ownership. SAM was able to save the rock formation, now the centerpieces of Enchanted Rock State Park, a part of the Texas Department of Parks and Wildlife, from being quarried.

Sept 2nd & 3d, in camp.

After his arrival at Highsmith's camp, Colonel Hays first action was to ask for volunteers to join the Pioneer Expedition from the Ranger company. Since the Rangers had been transferred from the control of the State of Texas to the U.S. military for the Mexican War, legally they were still in the United States Army, at least until December of 1848 when they would be mustered out. Under the circumstances, they might not have been true volunteers, but the thirty-five required for the exploration west, including Samuel Highsmith, were said to be eager to join their Mexican War leader, Jack Hays. Along with the Ranger volunteers, ten Delaware Indian scouts under John Conner's command were added to the final group. Although the Delaware Indians may not have been volunteers as were Highsmith's Rangers, the Delawares were the final addition to the group.

Sept. 4th, Up the Llano river 3 miles.

Sept. 5th, in camp.

With no explanation from Maverick as to why they stopped there, the members of the Expedition traveled three miles up the Llano River from the Ranger camp where they stayed for two days. It is fair to assume that the purpose was to organize the members into an expeditionary force, assigning duties to the complex group of individuals chosen to explore the border and to find a wagon route. Arms, ammunition, animals and supplies must have been distributed in preparation for the journey at this time. It would not be long before they entered an area through which most of the members had never traveled and little or nothing was known about the Indian tribes living there.

Sept. 6th, to mouth of Comanche creek.

Finally, on September 6th, 1848, the full complement of "50 armed men and 10 Delaware Indians" began the exploration by riding up the Llano River to camp at the mouth of Comanche Creek, where there was an Indian trail through the Texas Hill Country up to the San Saba River. The importance of Comanche Creek as an "Indian highway" led to the construction of Fort Mason at the junction of the east and west branches of the creek to provide protection for settlers in the region. However, in 1848 no permanent settlement had been established there, although Comanche Creek was the route by which Highsmith's Rangers returned home from Presidio del Norte.

Their camp at Comanche Creek was the first of many sites where they stopped during the Expedition and typical of how Rangers crossed the frontier. Walter Prescott Webb[28] described how they usually traveled in the following manner: "In moving across country, a company of Rangers traveled mainly in the daytime, usually sticking to the divides rather than to the established routes. They knew that practically all streams in Texas have a southeast course, and they seemed to be able to make their way without getting lost. They tried to camp on a stream, or by a waterhole. If they approached a stream, they would cross it before making camp to safeguard against a rise which might cut them off." Throughout the 1848 exploration the Expedition's approach to moving across the western lands remained much the same as described by Webb for the Rangers, except for the days when they were lost near the Rio Grande.

Sept. 7th, to James river - 4 miles above mouth.

From Comanche Creek, the expedition rode up the Llano to above the James River, near where the Llano Uplift ends as they re-entered the limestone formations of the Edwards Plateau, probably near Mill Creek. Then, traveling along the western side of the Blue Mountains to avoid a major canyon of the Llano River farther to the west, their route was over relatively flat land until it reached the Llano River just north of Junction, Texas . It may be surprising to many people, including native Texans, to learn that the confluence of the North and South Llano Rivers at Junction is very close to the geographic center of Texas, both east to west and north to south, even though Junction is 110 miles northwest of San Antonio.

Sept. 8th, to Llano again, 3 miles below mouth of S. fork.

Sam Maverick's entry, "below mouth of S. fork," refers to where the North and South Llano River meet at Junction. SAM could also have been referring to the south fork of a trail that the Spaniards had originally used for travel from the San Saba presidio/mission near Menard to the Nueces Canyon missions. The simplest route to the San Saba from the Llano River confluence was by way of the North Llano, then up Bear Creek and down Las Moras Creek to the presidio near Menard. The Expedition's route up the South Llano River to the old mission at Montell was almost certainly on an old Indian trail the Spaniards used for their trips between the missions.

Although an Indian or Spanish trail from the presidio/mission on the San Saba River south to the Nueces Canyon missions had been used as late as 1770 by Spaniards, it had been over seventy-five years after the missions outside of San Antonio were abandoned when the Pioneer Expedition traveled down the Nueces River trail toward Las Moras Springs. For many decades prior to the 1848 expedition, the Nueces Canyon had been the domain of several Indian tribes, most recently the Comanches.

Sept. 9th, to the Llano again near lake.

After camping just below the confluence of the South and North Llano Rivers, the Expedition rode up the broad valley of the South Llano to camp near what SAM called a "lake," although no lake can be found in this section of the river today. The original lake has probably been filled by progressive upstream erosion over many decades as the upstream lands were developed for farming and ranching. This day's campsite, close to where Bailey Creek enters the river, is just below the section of the South Llano River where the surrounding bluffs gradually enclose the riverbed, turning it into a sequence of springs flowing out of the Edwards Plateau, rather than a continuously flowing river.

Sept. 10th, to the farthest water up, viz: Paint Rock - 1/2 mile above spring.

Riding upriver, the expedition passed the junction of the South Llano and Big Paint Rock Creek which is where Sam Maverick made the entry, "Paint Rock." The reason for Maverick's comment is that a bluff on the east side is the site of Indian pictographs for which the creek was named. Maverick's observation and entry about the Indian Rock Art at this site is the earliest known record describing the presence of the pictographs in what Kirkland and Newcomb later called the "Lower Pecos River Region."[29] However, Forrest Kirkland's visit to the pictograph site at Maverick's "Paint Rock" was almost ninety years (1937) after the Pioneer Expedition. Unfortunately, by the time Kirkland documented the pictographs on the bluff above the South Llano, he stated that "almost every design has flaked off". Only one of the designs first noted by Sam Maverick was clearly distinguishable since many of the rocks had tumbled down from the bluff and still others had been scratched or painted over by visitors. Kirkland was able to paint and describe the rock art that was still visible in 1937, confirming Maverick's observation of Indian rock art in September, 1848. His ability to recognize Indian "Paint Rock" proved to be critical to this writer's locating part of the 1848 Pioneer Expedition's original trail.

The pictograph site that SAM called "Paint Rock" was downstream from the "farthest water up," so the campsite this day was probably a half-mile above the now famous "700 Springs" on the South Llano River. These springs arise from a long cleft in the western bluff above the riverbed and extend several hundreds yards along the river. From the clefts in the bluff, the springs flow down in spectacular fashion to a large pond, creating a beautiful, multi-colored display unlike any other springs seen on the Llano River. Even now, just as the earliest inhabitants of the region must have felt, a chance to visit and view "700 Springs" is well worth the effort required to reach the site.

This camp above 700 Springs was the Expedition's last in the South Llano River valley since the following day they rode up onto the "divide" separating the watersheds of the South Llano and Nueces Rivers. The divide, or watershed, between the two rivers is actually part of the broad, flat Edwards Plateau which extends from western Texas eastward to end in the Texas Hill Country. However, this section of the plateau between the river valleys is relatively small, even though its many springs still provide a reliable, year-round supply of water to the region. The availability of water and the plateau's open country with scattered stands of oak trees are why the Hill Country has long been a major ranching and hunting area in the State of Texas.

Sept 11th, It is 30 miles to head spring of Nueces - say this WSW 10 miles.

Sept. 12th, to head of North or Main Nueces. Say this day SW 20 miles.

The location of the September 11th campsite is difficult to determine since it was described by SAM in relation to the "head spring of Nueces." Their camp most likely was on the divide above Eagle Springs, the major source of water for the East Prong of the Nueces River. From there the trail would have followed the waterflow southwest down the East Prong to the

Nueces River Canyon where it joins Hackberry Creek to become the Nueces River.

Sept. 13th, Down the Nueces. We killed two or more of the six buffalos.

This day their ride down the canyon of the Nueces River was in a valley surrounded on both sides by steep hills. Fairly narrow through this section, the valley occasionally spreads out into broad, grassy plains where they must have found and killed the buffalos. Living off the land with adequate food and water for both men and animals was relatively simple in the Nueces Canyon.

What is remarkable about this comment is that buffalo were found living in the Nueces Canyon south of the Edwards Plateau. That location is at the same latitude as northern Coahuila in Mexico, powerful evidence that the Buffalo were south of their normal range on the High Plains. The weather must have been both cooler and more humid than those same lands are today, an effect of the Little Ice Age that gradually ended around 1850. No matter what the cause, today the lands around the Nueces Canyon are both drier and warmer (hotter?) than at the time of the 1848 Expedition.

Sept. 14th, to the old stone mission.

Sept. 15th, rested on the 15th - getting out of bread.

Based on the mileage traveled, the Expedition rested at the Nuestra Senora mission in Montell rather than at San Lorenzo near Camp Wood. Unfortunately, today not even one stone from the original mission can found at its location in Montell. Two churches, neither of them Catholic, and a cemetery have been built across the highway from the original mission. The beauty of the Canyon with the Nueces River close by readily explain why the missions were originally located in the river canyon.The first, San Lorenzo de la Santa Cruz, was built at Camp Wood and the second, Nuestra Senora de la Candelaria del Canon, at Montell.

Sept. 16th, to water hole a mile W of Nueces river.

After an extra day of rest at the old mission, they followed the Nueces down to camp at a waterhole west of where Haby Crosssing is now located. This location is several miles south of the Nueces Canyon and almost due east of Las Moras Springs in the flat lands south of the Edwards Plateau.

Sept 17th, to head of Las Moras Cr., Total 285 miles.

Finally, on September 17th, the company of fifty armed men and ten Delaware Indians arrived at Las Moras Springs. The Springs were both the end of the first phase and the starting point for the westward exploration. Besides their physical beauty and abundant supply of water, the Springs had special significance for Maverick since they were now his property. Using the headright earned fighting for the Republic of Texas, SAM had claimed one 320 acre tract at Las Moras Springs and another 320 acres around the mouth of Las Moras Creek at the Rio Grande.[23] In September 1848, the Springs were the meeting place for the expeditionary force, led by Jack Hays, that would explore the American lands along the Texas-Mexico border while seeking a wagon road route from San Antonio to Chihuahua and El Paso del Norte, with a group from San Antonio searching for possible mining sites.

However, Las Moras Springs had greater significance than as a meeting place to start the exploration. Although SAM did not include in his journal, probably because so little was known about their trails in western Texas, Las Moras Springs and Creek were on a major Comanche trail that they traveled to raid South Texas and the northern states of Mexico. U.S. Army reconnaissances following the 1848 Hays exploration would find that the Comanche trail through Las Moras was one of two major routes into Mexico. What the U.S. Army at the time did not know was how to stop their raids in Texas and Mexico.

The Army knew that the Comanches were expert horse warriors, but in 1848 the U.S. infantry had no resources capable of controlling or preventing their attacks south of the springs . In 1852, as one of its first steps in preventing those raids, the United States Army leased the springs and creek from Sam Maverick where Fort Clark, a cavalry post, was built so immediate responses to raids by the Comanches and other tribes were possible. Fort Clark was maintained as a cavalry post until its closure in 1944 during World War II, long after the Comanches had been moved to their reservation in Oklahoma.

The Old Spanish Missions

Originally, the Spanish missions built by the Roman Catholic Church in Texas were located close to presidios garrisoned with Spanish soldiers to protect the missions. From the first mission in 1682 until the last in 1793, missions were built at forty different sites, lasting from less than a year to over a century.[30] The original goal was to serve the dual function of pacifying the Indian tribes while providing protection for settlers along the frontier. During the initial period of their existence, the emphasis was on converting the natives to the Christian faith at the missions, but this phase was gradually replaced by the increasing demands on the Spanish government to protect its rights in Texas and the bordering territories.

In early April 1757, and after an extended period of negotiations, a joint expedition supported by both Franciscan friars and the Spanish government left San Antonio for a location on the San Saba River near today's Menard, Texas to establish a combination mission-presidio for the purpose of converting the Lipan Apaches and establishing a permanent Spanish settlement. Although no Apaches were found when the expedition finally arrived at the San Saba site, a mission, Santa Cruz de San Saba, and the presidio, Presidio San Luis de las Amarillas, were built three miles apart. Unfortunately, the mission failed to attract even one Apache convert during the following year and rapidly became the target of the Apaches' enemies who converged on the mission in early March 1758. Despite a request from the presidio to move its people there for protection, none were moved and on March 18, 1758, the Comanches and their allies attacked the mission, killing many of its occupants and most of the animals before setting fire to the buildings and stealing everything of value. Santa Cruz de San Saba would become the only Texas mission destroyed by an Indian attack and never rebuilt.

The presidio continued to be garrisoned by the Spanish government for ten more years despite repeated Indian attacks, one of which was supported by the French. However, the missionary activities were never re-instituted since the Apaches would not be pacified despite the Spaniards efforts to protect them from their bitter enemies to the north. Even after its commander, Rabago, increased his efforts to make peace with the hostile tribes, the presidio continued to suffer from Indian attacks, including their intercepting supplies from San Antonio for the garrison. In an attempt to satisfy a Lipan Apache chief, Rabago established a mission, San Lorenzo de la Santa Cruz, near today's Camp Wood on the Nueces River in January 1762 with a guard of twenty men. At the request of another Lipan chief, an additional mission, Nuestra Senora de la Candelaria del Canon, was built ten miles south of the first mission in the Nueces River canyon with ten additional soldiers from the presidio. The shift to the new missions weakened the defense of the San Saba presidio and all three sites were repeatedly attacked by the Comanches, which would lead to the demise of both the presidio and the two missions.

When the Marques de Rubi, who had been ordered to inspect the northern presidios in August 1764, finally arrived at the San Saba presidio and the Nueces Canyon missions, he found them to be in dire straits and in his report would recommend their closing. In June 1768, Rabago moved from the San Saba to mission San Lorenzo from which he was removed from its command for possible treason. After another feeble attempt to reoccupy the San Saba presidio, the site was permanently abandoned in 1770. In 1771, the Nueces Canyon missions were also closed with their soldiers dispersed to San Antonio and a new mission south of the Rio Grande.

After completing his inspection in November 1767, Rubi recommended that the presidential defenses be reorganized below a "real" frontier stretching from the Gulf of California to the mouth of the Guadalupe River in Texas with fifteen presidios approximately a hundred miles apart. Only the Santa Fe and San Antonio presidios north of the new frontier should be protected and all Spanish activities in East Texas abandoned. Almost five years later, King Charles III gave a royal order known as the "New Regulations for Presidios" that required closing all missions and presidios in Texas, except for those at San Antonio and La Bahia, with San Antonio being strengthened and designated the capitol of the province. Rubi's recommendations had finally become a royal edict, effectively ending Spanish settlement in Texas. Although Spain continued to govern the region until Mexico won its independence, the stage had been set for the gradual settlement of Texas by Anglo-Americans moving into the state from the east.

The closing of the Nueces Canyon missions in 1771, over three-quarters of a century before the Pioneer Expedition camped at the site of Nuestra Senora de la Candelaria del Canon, was one of the final events of the Spanish Mission era as Spanish governance gradually disappeared from

Texas, leaving behind its many legacies. The Pioneer Expedition's westward exploration in 1848 was the first step taken by the United States government to establish control over the lands west of central Texas. The problems responsible for the Nueces Canyon missions' original construction as well as their abrupt closure must have been known to the Pioneer Expedition members. Those problems were still present when the Expedition started its exploration of the *terra incognita* of western Texas, lands that neither Spain nor Mexico had been able to settle or control.

4

Westward to La Junta De Los Rios / The River Canyon Country

The Pioneer Expedition's arrival at Las Moras Springs was both an end and a start. It was the end of preparations because the members, supplies and animals required for the exploration had been assembled, although the process had required three weeks of the two months scheduled for the Expedition. It was also the end of travel through explored lands because their route to Las Moras Springs had been over a north-south trail that had been used by native tribes since before construction of the Spanish missions in Nueces Canyon.

The springs were the starting place of the Expedition from which it departed into a *terra incognita* which had been inhabited by both indigenous and nomadic tribes for many centuries. Compared to how long native tribes had lived there, its exploration and limited settlement by the Spain had been little more than transient. The Expedition's route to Chihuahua and El Paso would be from east to west in a region where the existing trails in the new American territories had been almost exclusively north-south, either as Indian trails or as trade routes between Mexico and its northern settlements. The 1848 Pioneer Expedition would be the first American exploration of the new Texas-Mexico border from the Devils River up to La Junta de los Rios (Presidio del Norte), although the original objective had been El Paso del Norte. The description of the exploration that follows is based on Sam Maverick's original 1848 journal after editing by his son-in-law, Edwin H. Terrell (E.H.T.).

East of San Antonio where the "Old Three Hundred" first settled in Texas, the terrain varies from rolling plains to flatlands covered with grass except for the fields being prepared for planting. Tall trees grow along the banks of several flowing creeks that cut across the plains. An occasional large river in a broad, flat floodplain collects water from the creeks on its way to the Gulf of Mexico. Members of the 1848 Chihuahua-El Paso Pioneer Expedition, the first American expedition to explore the new border with Mexico, had lived in and traveled those relatively flat, eastern lands with an abundant water supply. Few of them had been west of Del Rio along the Rio Grande where they would search for a wagon road route from San Antonio to Chihuahua and El Paso.

The trail of the 1848 Pioneer Expedition, as Sam Maverick described in the only record of the exploration, was through much different terrain than the eastern region of Texas,. The first section of the trail to San Felipe Creek had been through or near the Hill Country, a region with many sources of water despite its flat topography. Even west of the Nueces River, the route to the Rio Grande was through rolling countryside with many springs and creeks flowing down from the Hill Country. However, the topography changed in and around the Devils River where their travels were so difficult that their leader, the legendary Texas Ranger, Colonel Jack Hays, gave the river the name that persists to this day. What the 1848 Pioneer Expedition members quickly learned was that the Rio Grande borderlands were so dry, rugged and complex that no similar topography could have been found elsewhere in the State.

The formation of the borderlands began over 140 million years ago at the start of the Cretaceous period. As the continents separated, an inland sea was created extending from the Arctic Ocean to the Gulf of Mexico, covering most of Texas. During the Early Cretaceous time, skeletons of calcareous organisms were deposited on the sea's floor as a homogeneous mixture of carbonates, i.e., limestone and dolomite, but during the Late Cretaceous period, the deposits became more heterogeneous with less marine and more organic material. Then, about 65 millions years ago during the Early Tertiary period, increased tectonic activity forced the ancient Ouachita Mountains below the Cretaceous limestone into a collision with the Laramide orogeny (Rocky Mountains), uplifting the buried limestone at the Big Bend. Over the next millions of years, compression alternated with relaxation of the earth's crust, creating rifts from which volcanic ash exploded and lava flowed, ultimately burying the entire Big Bend region with volcanic ash and debris thousands of feet deep. Below thi mass of volcanic material lay today's boundary between Texas and Mexico, the Rio Grande / Rio Bravo.

The current course of the Rio Grande was created as described by Donald McGookey in *Geologic Wonders of West Texas*:[31, p. 140] "During the Late Tertiary (from Early Miocene time on), broad uplift of the area and the accompanying rifting resulted in the removal by erosion of thousands of feet of rock. Many cubic miles of eroded rock was transported by the Rio Grande to the Gulf of Mexico basin. It was during this time that the course of the Rio Grande was superimposed (eroded down into = entrenched) across uplifted blocks and anticlines. By the end of the Oligocene Epoch, the Big Bend area was covered by volcanic debris of all kinds that was extremely thick and extended far beyond the present distribution. Some have estimated that the cover was five times the thickness we see today. River systems were established draining generally from west to east with some major bends around the primary extrusive centers. As the area was uplifted, the rivers became entrenched (deepened their channels) and continued to follow the same course as layer upon layer of volcanic debris, and then underlying sediments, were stripped away by erosion. In this manner, the rivers were superimposed to follow previous courses over structurally low and high areas. Thus, we now see deep canyons cutting across mountains of hard limestone and wonder why they didn't take the easy way around one end or the other of the mountain trend."

After removal of volcanic debris, two vast carbonate plateaus (Edwards, Stockton) extended from the Balcones Escarpment at the east end to the volcanic fields of Big Bend at the west end. The terrain of those plateaus is classical karst topography, which is "an irregular topography characterized by sinkholes, caverns and lack of surface streams in humid regions because an underlying carbonate formation has been riddled with underground drainage channels that capture the surface streams."[32] Despite the eastern end of the Edwards Plateau (Hill Country) meeting the criteria for karst terrain, that part of the plateau has an adequate water runoff (one-ten inches/square mile annually),[33] primarily due to a greater annual rainfall, so its surface streams usually provides enough water for its human and animal inhabitants. Members of the 1848 Pioneer Expedition had traveled through the Hill Country many times, and even after a ride up the Llano River and down the Nueces River to Las Moras Springs, they had no reason to be concerned about sources of water during the exploration.

However, the western end of the Edwards Plateau and the Stockton Plateau are classical "karst terrain" with caves, caverns, sinkholes, springs and *tinajas*, but no major surface rivers (due to less than one inch/square mile of annual runoff). In fact, from west of its confluence with the Pecos River up to the Rio Conchos junction (La Junta de los Rios), the Rio Grande is the only perennially flowing river or stream in the region. The only additional water flow entering the river comes either from periodic rainstorms or from underground water released from aquifers. In the 21st Century, the Rio Grande flows past one canyon or draw after another on both the American and Mexican sides of the river upstream from Del Rio to Presidio, Texas. Despite hundreds of canyons created over millions of years by multiple geological changes, no reliable supply of flowing water exists other than the Rio Grande. For that reason, the name, River Canyon Country, has been given to the lands surrounding the Rio Grande from Del Rio upstream to La Junta de los Rios.

The barren River Canyon Country west of the Pecos River, without adequate sources of surface water as in the Hill Country, was a vast region with few if any permanent residents. However, as Joseph H. Labadie, a retired National Park Service archeologist, has stated in reference to the Lower Pecos Region,[34] "surface water was the magnet that drew people to the area. Where you have a steady supply of water you also have stable populations of plants and animals. The presence of three river valleys with permanent water supplies in a roughly one hundred square mile area made this region a biotic paradise since the end of the last Ice Age some 12,000 years ago." The permanent water supply explains why humans have lived around the confluence of the three rivers for thousands of years, leaving behind a treasure trove of Rock Art that has survived into the 21st Century.

The 1848 Chihuahua-El Paso Pioneer Expedition was the first Anglo-American exploration of the River Canyon Country, the most scenic and incredibly complex terrain in the State of Texas,. While exploring the new borderlands, the 1848 expedition rode in and along the Rio Grande just as prehistoric humans had walked before the arrival of Europeans. However, the 1848 exploration of the River Canyon Country ended at San Francisco Creek, the route by which they left the Rio Grande to become the first Americans to explore Big Bend National Park. The Lower Canyons of the Rio Grande from Boquillas Canyon down to San Francisco Canyon, that is, the east side of the Big Bend, are too deep and rugged even for travel with horses and mules. Thus, the exploration of that section, created by more complex geological changes than those that created the country through which the Pioneer expedition had ridden, would not be completed until the Boundary Survey by Mexico and the United States several years later.

In addition to the complex topography produced by tectonic activity, prehistoric inhabitants contributed to what makes the River Canyon

Country a unique region in the United States. Those ancient peoples left evidence of their cultures in the form of thousands of pictographs, petroglyphs, camping sites and ancient artifacts that produced one of the richest archeological sites in the world. Unfortunately, the ancient treasures on both sides of the Rio Grande/Rio Bravo have never been adequately inventoried or studied. Our locating a previously undiscovered prehistoric camping site in Sanderson Canyon is powerful evidence that more sites and artifacts remain to be discovered. Unfortunately, evidence of the inhabitants' thousands of years of life along the Rio Grande, especially in the River Canyon Country, is gradually disappearing and may never be accurately described before natural processes destroy those prehistoric sites.

Las Moras Springs To Lower Pecos River Canyon

With its departure from Las Moras Springs on September 19, 1848, the Chihuahua-El Paso Pioneer Expedition became the first American effort to locate the trails, rivers, mountain ranges, peaks and watersheds found in the lands which extend west from central Texas and north of the Rio Grande. Sam Maverick's journal briefly describes their route through those lands which were, and are, the most isolated and desolate in all of Texas. The obstacles that the Expedition encountered while exploring the River Canyon Country, and how its members survived those travels, is a story about what a remarkable group of men was able to accomplish over 160 years ago.

> *Sept. 18th, Monday. Rested at spring of the Las Moras Cr. Col. Evertson, Dr. Sturgess & Co. come to us here on a mining expedition etc.*

With the arrival from San Antonio of Colonel Evertson, Doctor Sturgess and their group to search for possible silver or gold mines, the Pioneer Expedition was ready to travel west to the Rio Grande and the Devil's River, most commonly called the Puerco at the time. In addition, the first few days on the Trail was over countryside not much different than the lands between Las Moras and San Antonio. Since the Hill Country was north of the trail, no major hills or divides similar to those of the Edwards Plateau had to be climbed. Water for the men and their horses was easily found in the creeks or springs between Las Moras and the Devil's River.

Forage for their animals in those days was probably more than adequate for the large group of men and animals. So the Expedition headed west from Las Moras Springs expecting a relatively easy journey to Chihuahua and on to El Paso before their return to San Antonio.

> *Sept 19th, We cross Maverick's Creek one and a half miles above its mouth and camp on San Pedro Cr. - Dream of my poor dear Tita and of Augusta and Mary.*
>
> *Sept 20th, Camp on Turkey Cr. 1 1/2 miles below Sugar loaf (N. 10 degrees E. of camp).*
>
> *Sept 21st, Mouth of Devil's river.*
> *(N.B. this is the spelling for the river which SAM first recorded and will be used throughout the text despite the current elimination of the apostrophe.)*

Sam Maverick's entry on September 19th about his dreams at the Sycamore Creek camp reflects the agonizing grief he felt over the loss of his daughters as well as how much he missed his wife, Mary.[1] Although Hays had convinced Mary that SAM's grief was the reason why his old friend should join the exploration, other factors were also important. Maverick's public stature and expertise as a surveyor/attorney brought credibility few others could bring. Besides that, SAM had explored many areas of Texas in the past and was experienced in dealing with the many dangers they would face. However, the brevity of his notes and comments compared to his earlier journals clearly show that Maverick's mental state was different than during his early travels.

Riding west, the group crossed first Maverick's Creek and camped on San Pedro (now Sycamore) Creek, a site which would become a stop on the Chihuahua Road that the Expedition sought. After an overnight camp on Turkey Creek, now named San Felipe Creek for its source springs at Del Rio, Texas, they rode up a trail along the Rio Grande to the confluence of the Devil's River with the Rio Grande. Today the "mouth of the Devil's River" is two to three hundred yards above Lake Amistad's dam and approximately two hundred feet below the surface. Needless to say, this was not a campsite we re-explored, even if we could have located the site.

>Sept 22nd, *Camp on N.W. side of same at remarkable ford in hills - beaver - going say 5 miles E.. & N.E. and 10 miles N. & N.W.*

When one reads September 22nd entry in SAM's journal, the first question that comes to mind is: why did they travel east and northeast, then north and northwest, if the goal was to find a trail to the west? The probable explanation is that they followed the Devil's River across its floodplain, now under the waters of Lake Amistad. Their first campsite above the Devil's mouth fits a location close to Rough Canyon, the eastern bluff which appears to rise out of the lake water as if it were a giant ship afloat in the lake when approached from the south.

>Sept 22nd.

The bluffs at and above Rough Canyon, rising four to five hundred feet above the riverbed, mark the eastern edge of the River Canyon Country. The Devil's River floodplain was the last they would cross until they reached the eastern end of La Junta de los Rios, the floodplain of the Rio Concho/Rio Grande junction. The difficulties they encountered trying to travel up the Devil's riverbed were what led Jack Hays to name the river, the "Devil's River." It was not long before Hays and the other Expedition members found that the Devil's was far from the worst such river or canyon through, or across which, they had to ride, but the Devil's, you might say, introduced the group to the problems created by the difficult terrain of the River Canyon Country.

>Sept 23rd, *Going 8 miles N.E., then 5 miles in horrid ravine to Devil's river for water.*

SAM's brief entries poorly reflect how difficult the ride up or along the Devil's must have been, except for his describing a "horrid ravine." Hays was said to have complained about the number of crossings required to ride up the river, but the problem is even worse above Baker's Crossing on the Devil's River.

After a very difficult ride in the ravine, the Expedition camped near Indian Springs on the Devil's just below where the river takes a sharp turn back to the southwest. All that can be seen up the river from this campsite are a series of bluffs, one after another, a much different topography from any Texas river that the Expedition members were likely to have seen elsewhere in Texas.

Sept 24th, *Up Devil's river, leading our horses.*

Obviously, this part of the Devil's River must have been very rough, with many boulders in the riverbed, as in others parts of the Devil's since the Expedition members, all of whom were expert horsemen, had to lead their horses up and around the sharp bend where the river's upstream course turns from northeast to southwest. Even worse, once around the bend, the Expedition was again faced with high bluffs above the river on both sides. Only two breaks in the bluffs can be found upstream along this section of the river before it turns again back to the north. The break on the right, Satan's Canyon, is relatively large but also flows back to the north and northeast. On the left a broaddraw with an arm extending upward to the west gradually drains down to the river. This draw must have been where the Expedition left the Devil's River since it has relatively easy access and the distance from their last camp agrees with an exit from the Devil's at this site.

Sept 25th, *Going W.N.W. Camp on Pecos divide without water. DeLacey's sickness and delay.*

After making only three miles the previous day, the Expedition's rode an unusually long distance (25 miles) out of the Devil's River watershed up to the divide which separates the Devil's from the Pecos River valley. Camping on a divide without any water is no surprise because the divide, over which Ranch Road 1024 now runs, is still dry today except during rainstorms. Windmills were the first devices which could provide a reliable water supply on or near the divide . But in 1848 no water from a spring or creek, much less from a windmill, was available and the Pecos River, deep in its canyon to the west, could not be seen from the divide. This camp was the first of many "dry camps" since the camp's location was in a region of Texas which was and is completely different from any other part of Texas.

Sept 26th, *To the Pecos- in great thirst.*

No direction, just the mileage (15 miles), was described in SAM's entry for September 26th, but to have reached the Pecos within the mileage recorded, the men had to ride almost due west from the divide. Although two or three routes could have been used for entry into the Pecos River Canyon, the most likely site was an entry into Lewis Canyon above its junction with the Pecos. The ride down into the canyon should have been relatively easy and, since the Pecos backs up into Lewis Canyon, water should have been quickly available for men – in great thirst. The junction with the Pecos River also offered a comfortable location on the Pecos River where a large company of men can easily camp.

The Lewis Canyon petroglyphs created by Early Americans are located on a flat limestone bluff above this campsite[35] and could not have been seen by the Expedition's members unless scouts found them while exploring along the Pecos. The surface material covering the petroglyphs has been excavated by archeologists and the Rock Art Foundation since their discovery in the 1930s. Although the Expedition's members were the first Anglo-Americans to explore the region, their arrival was centuries later than the Early American rock artists who had created the petroglyphs.

Sept 27th, *Out again among the hills & ravines, zig-zag - going not more than 5 miles. Traveling nine hours hard over rocks to the Pecos again.*

Little has changed since 1848 where travel on horses and mules in the lower canyons of the Pecos River is concerned. Floating down the Pecos and fishing the river is a safe and pleasurable activity, as Louis Aulbach has shown, but these days riding horses with pack mules up the Pecos River from Lewis Canyon would still be "hard over rocks" with little daily progress up the Pecos. The shear, high bluffs above the Pecos are almost continuous on both sides compared to the periodic breaks in the Devil's River and even the few openings rise sharply from the riverbed. The "hills & ravines, zig-zag" described by Maverick must have been on the right or eastern side of the Pecos because the left or western side is a smooth, sheer bluff rising sharply above the river.

Sept 28th, *In camp. Evertson with us again. Total 418 miles.*

As previously noted, the Devil's River and Pecos River presented problems to Jack Hays and his fellow leaders which they had not faced in their earlier Texas travels. The lower canyons of both rivers meander, that is, following a winding and twisting course, a characteristic of rivers flowing across level lands in sedimentary basins similar to the lower Mississippi River basin. Exploration above the confluence of the Pecos River and Lewis Canyon should have revealed to the scouts that the Pecos River turned back to the east a few miles above their camp, blocking further travel to the west or north. The Devil's River bluffs had already created a similar problem for the Expedition due to the river's turning sharply back to the southwest.

The meanders of the lower Pecos River-Rio Grande, Devil's River may be explained by the observation that the two rivers along with the drainages from Mexico downstream from Del Rio are the oldest through-flowing rivers in the Rio Concho-Rio Grande-Pecos River basin. In reference to the meandering river canyons of the Colorado Plateau, Hunt[33] noted that present-day meanders of those canyons are poorly understood and must represent ancient features that have been modified as canyon cutting progressed, almost certainly the same process that created the modern-day Rio Grande topography. Perhaps, as in the Snake River Basin, the Pecos and Devil's flowed over a relatively flat sedimentary basin before the region was uplifted, eroding through the bedrock barriers to form high cliffs as the lands rose.

Sept 29th, *Cross 1/2 mile below and go up crawling like flies, on side of mountain, gaining not over 200 yards.*

Despite the difficulties the Expedition had already faced, Hays chose to climb out of the Pecos River canyon to the west side and continue their exploration of the U.S.-Mexico border. Despite traveling (climbing?) three miles on the 29th, that day's campsite was only 200 yards from the previous day's site, which could only have been on the bluff opposite the Pecos River camp. Despite SAM's describing their climb upward as "crawling like flies, on side of mountain," the bluffs are only 200 to 300 feet above the river in this part of the canyon, but the climb for men with horses and pack mules must have been extremely arduous, no matter where they climbed up to the top of the bluff.

The difficulty of the climb out of the river's canyon to continue the exploration was obviously enough to convince "Colonel Evertson," who had just re-joined the group, to return to San Antonio. Upon arriving home, he was quoted as saying that the Expedition's members could not survive further exploration westward, an observation that almost proved to be true.

> Sept 30th, *Take new small trail and in 4 miles come into trail which suppose crosses Pecos about 4 miles above camp. Camp without water. Going S.W. and then S.*

After an extra day camping in the lower Pecos River canyon (28th) and a very difficult climb up a western bluff of the river canyon on the 29th, the Expedition rode southwest toward the Rio Grande along a route northwest of present day Langtry, Texas. Determining the expedition's exact route through the Langtry area is difficult, but both Eagle's Nest and Langtry Creeks had to be crossed based on SAM's recorded mileage and direction. The location of their "camp without water" was significant because it was the first of several sites where they camped on or near the Rio Grande while exploring the new Texas-Mexico border. SAM's comment "without water" indicates that the campsite was not on the river or a creek or adjacent to a waterhole. As such, a location on a ridge above Rattlesnake Canyon would be a typical Ranger camp, i.e. after crossing Langtry Creek and on a divide.[28]

Based on SAM's entry for the day, the Expedition must have followed a major Indian trail from their camp above the Pecos River down to a ridge above the Rio Grande. In fact, the trail probably extended northward from the Rio Grande to the Pecos River which it crossed near Pandale, Texas into Howard's Draw. Recently, Aulbach and Enos (personal communication) confirmed that evidence of Indian habitation at Rattlesnake Canyon, specifically lithic points, on the bluff above the river. Thus, the Expedition's campsite above Rattlesnake Canyon was more than its first camp near the Rio Grande. The campsite was also the first where the group documented the existence of a major Indian crossing into Mexico west of the Devil's River.

Never A Despoblado by Joseph H. Labadie

The Pioneer Expedition of 1848 is among the first well-documented journeys into this region undertaken by Anglo Americans following Texas entry into the Union. The rock shelters and river terraces of the Pecos and Devil's Rivers lower canyons harbor an unparalleled record of human prehistory that spans nearly 12,000 years and contain some of the densest concentrations of prehistoric rock art in the New World. The Expedition traversed a region that is today considered to be among the world's greatest prehistoric rock art regions—comparable to Europe, Australia, and America's Baja California.

Sam Maverick's journal may be relatively silent on the subject, but he undoubtedly encountered, on a daily basis, the remains of prehistoric campfire pits, pictographs, well-worn trails, and debris left by prehistoric cultures. What did the Expedition's members think of all this— they obviously knew that they were among the first Anglo Americans to see this barren landscape firsthand? Did they actually meet some of the region's aboriginal residents and purposefully omit the encounter from the daily journal? Maverick's journal contains some titillating entries on such matters, but is silent on many of the most asked questions by modern day researchers. What they want to know is more about the Native Americans who obviously watched the Expedition make its way through their homeland.

Today we know that the pictographs (Native American paintings on rock surfaces and cave walls) that Sam Maverick saw and mentioned in his journal are among the largest multicolored images in North America: some reach more than 13 feet (4m) tall; some are clustered in panels extending over 100 feet (20m) along the rear walls of rock shelters. Maverick undoubtedly noticed the astonishing preservation of the archeological materials in the region's many dry rock shelters, possibly stopping to observe but not mention them in his journal. Even if no descriptions of the pictographs were included, the Expedition no doubt got more than a little help in determining where to cross a river or creek, where to look for food or water, and where to pitch a camp by following the signs of those Native Americans that had come before them.

We know today that there are four major prehistoric and several historic pictograph styles represented in the region's many sites, with the oldest style tentatively dated back to roughly 4000 years before present. The styles can be arranged in chronological order, beginning with the elaborate, polychrome Pecos River style which is generally thought to be between 3500 to 4000 years old. The miniature Red Linear pictographs are probably more recent, but their span may overlap with the older style. The two latest prehistoric styles, the Red Monochrome and the Bold Line Geometrics, are believed to date back to a time after A.D. 600 but before A.D. 1600. Some historic pictographs, painted in a style characteristic of the Plains Indians, have the potential to be more precisely dated, but cannot be assigned to any specific group or to any modern day tribe of Native Americans.

Nor is it likely that any exact translation of rock art symbols into our frame of reference will ever be within our reach. Likewise we may never be able to fully appreciate or understand the supernatural world of the aboriginal mind of the peoples that once inhabited this region. The people and the culture that produced these pictographs are extinct. They left no written language and have no known modern descendants among existing Native American groups. Thus, the real meanings, functions, and purposes of the images are lost forever.

Many other questions about the prehistoric Native American groups that once inhabited the canyon lands and plateaus of the lower Pecos and Devil's river valleys also remain unanswered. For instance, what were the tribal identities, alliances, and enemies? And what did the people call themselves? No familiar American Indian names are mentioned in documents until the influx of Plains Indian groups in historic times such as the Apache and Comanches after the Great Pueblo Revolt of 1680 in New Mexico. With the diminishing presence and eventual dissolution of the Spanish empire in the region (1821) the Comanche, Kiowa, and other Plains groups asserted their dominance throughout the entire region traversed by the Pioneer Expedition in 1848. In some publications, the late prehistoric peoples of the area are referred to as "Coahuiltecans" based on similarities in life ways and material culture, but this designation only implies that they probably belonged to the same language group as other hunter-gatherer groups encountered in southern Texas and northeastern Mexico at the time of the first European contact.

One way we can make some inferences about the life ways of the Native American groups that lived the region where the Expedition traveled is by comparing their hunting and subsistence technologies, as evidenced by the artifacts they left behind, with living or documented groups in similar arid environments in Africa, Australia, and South America. Such comparisons, known as ethnographic analogies, suggest that prehistoric groups in this region were relatively small in number and thinly distributed across the region in order to exploit seasonal or geographic resources without seriously depleting them. The basic social unit would probably have been the extended family—a small, highly mobile group drawn together by ties of kinship. Familial relationships would serve to further the unity of the group, increasing cooperation through familiarity and affection. Other members might be attracted by the success of some individual or simple compatibility. Group composition would be fluid, permitting any friction to be resolved by members simply moving to another band. Protecting a nomadic life, these small groups could make seasonal rounds, harvesting plant foods as they ripened or moving when local supplies were diminished or hard to find in comparison to the amount of effort it took to satisfy group needs.

During time of relative abundance, for example, when desert fruits such as persimmons, mesquite beans, pecans, walnuts, and prickly pear cactus ripened, the dispersed families could congregate for communal harvests and celebrations. The need for exogamy—the rule of marrying outside the group—could be satisfied at these seasonal meetings. A forum for the exchange of information could be provided, and political ties could be formed or cemented at such gatherings. It seems probable that much of the region's most elaborate pictographs were painted as part of rituals enacted during periods when normally dispersed families congregated.

Traditionally, men would have controlled the hunting of larger animals, although the gathering of plant resources by women may have contributed more to the daily diet; the literally ate everything that didn't try to eat them first. The manufacture of more complex stone tools may well have been a task more commonly associated with men if ethnographic analogies are to be believed. The production of the finest projectile points used as spear and dart points involved labor and skill that goes far beyond that needed to produce an efficient weapon. Such an expenditure of time and effort to produce such an esthetically pleasing tool must have carried psychological or social rewards beyond the sheer utility of the object.

In all human societies, some able members of the group fulfill the need for leadership, although the degree to which power can be exercised corresponds to the population density and the resources to be controlled.

In an area such as Maverick traveled, where both people and basic commodities were sparse and unevenly dispersed across the landscape, a leader would probably rise to the top during times when organization was needed for a specific task. Examples might include the direction of a communal hunt by the most able hunter, or the leading of a raid or defending a camp by the bravest warrior. It is interesting to note that many historic Southern Plans and Northern Mexican bands and groups had both war and peace leaders, based upon the principle that the one most qualified to fight may not have been the best advocate of reconciliation or peace. Because the headman's power was simply a matter of acknowledged ability, high social status or rank was probably not hereditary, nor was it endowed with all encompassing control over the rest of their society. Often such a leader may have functioned only during his prime, to be later replaced by another, more competitive and able person. The elderly were not without merit, their experience and wisdom must have been sought during times of stress or group discordance.

The oldest and most widespread form of religious thought in North America, known as shamanism, is found among hunter-gather societies throughout the world. In this tradition, the shaman — or one who controls power or magic — was charged with the general welfare of the group or some other specific aspect of group society. The shaman was probably among the most powerful single individuals in the group. Shamans controlled the supernatural powers that permeated and affected every aspect of their physical, ideological, and social worlds — which were often inseparable. As magician, healer, or divinatory of the future through their special relationship with the supernatural world, the shaman were thought to be able to affect the success of an upcoming hunt or battle, cast spells to enchant people and animals, and communicate with the spirits that controlled the universe. As the most learned person in the group, they served as a storehouse of oral tradition, stories, myths, and facts about the group's history in relation to the order of the universe.

Many modern day researchers have speculated that the pictographs that Sam Maverick saw during his journey may have functioned as mnemonic devices — images used by shamans and storytellers to recall or remember specific events, people, or myths that were part of the group's oral histories. In many respects, the shaman would have been a teacher, relating his accumulated knowledge to the younger members of the group.

On an even more practical level, the shaman would have been an herbalist, curing disease through a combination of real and magical treatments. The most obvious evidence for the role of the shamanism in the region are the Pecos River style pictographs. These complex and elaborate artworks are considered by many researchers to be shamanic works—perhaps visions achieved in trance and then made permanent on the walls of the canyons by painted images.

Sam Maverick's journal suggests that he believed the peoples that left behind the artifacts and artworks he saw were "primitive" peoples. The ancient peoples of this region were primitive only in sense that the a modern day dictionary defines primitive as "relating to the earliest age or period." The lives of these ancient peoples could never be considered primitive in the sense of being inefficient, impoverished, or unfulfilling. The pictographs for which the region is most noted for today testify to a complex ideological or mythological world far more varied than their economic and technological remains suggest. By adapting to their environment, learning to utilize rather than drastically alter the natural resources, the native peoples of the lower Pecos and Devil's river canyon lands and plateaus were able to endure for the impressive time span of over 12,000 years before being absorbed or assimilated into the new cultures that came into the region.

The paradox of the Pioneer Expedition of 1848 is that it represents one of the first Anglo American groups to traverse and map the region. Their eyes were clearly focused on its use by future generations. On the other hand, the people who were undoubtedly there, but not mentioned by name in Sam Maverick's journal, were among the last whose eyes were collectively focused on a legacy that had endured for millennia. Neither group had any idea of what the future would bring.

Author's Comments:

Joe Labadie, who has lived in and studied the Lower Pecos Region for over 25 years, leaves little doubt that what the Spaniards had called *La Tierra Despoblada* had been home to many different native cultures who were far from primitive. Their Rock Art, religion, stone tools and complex diets were created thousands of years before the City of Rome was founded in Italy. Citizens of the 21st Century are fortunate that so much of what those early inhabitants developed has been preserved to see. Perhaps the time has come when more intensive study of the culture of those early inhabitants should be initiated so that we can learn more about what lies ahead for the world in which we live.

Up The Rio Grande to Sanderson Canyon

Having already traveled 418 miles with minimal success, September 28, 1848 must have been a day of decision for the Expedition leaders, especially Jack Hays. That day they were faced with three possible alternatives as to how to continue the exploration. The first was to return to San Antonio immediately, admitting that the Pioneer Expedition had been a failure. That is what Hays old friend and colleague, Colonel Evertson, chose to do, bringing back news to San Antonio that the members of the Expedition were almost certain to perish on their way to Chihuahua. The second choice was to ride back down the Pecos River to Lewis Canyon and take the relatively easy route up to the Pecos divide camp. From the divide, the Expedition could ride northward, searching for a road to Chihuahua and El Paso del Norte by a more northern route.

Instead, Hays chose to have the Expedition climb up the high bluff opposite their Lower Pecos Canyon campsite and travel southwest down to the Rio Grande. A story has been told for many years that a guide named Lorenzo, who had lived with the Comanches, claimed to know the route west to Chihuahua but didn't, resulting in the Expedition's getting lost. However, when the U.S. Government's commitment to prevent Indian incursions into Mexico, according to the Treaty of Guadalupe Hidalgo, is considered, Hays may have decided on the third alternative because of a commitment he made before the Expedition's departure from San Antonio. The U.S. Government did not know where the Rio Grande was, now the official border between Mexico and the United States, nor where the crossings used for Indian incursions into Mexico were located.

The search for the border and the Indian crossings resulted in the Pioneer Expedition members suffering in ways few could have imagined before they left Las Moras. Their route in the River Canyon Country between present-day Langtry and La Junta de los Rios is through the driest, highest and most difficult terrain in the State of Texas. It is no surprise that the exploration along the Rio Grande required much more time than originally planned and turned the Pioneer Expedition into a life-threatening undertaking.

Oct 1st, *Go to water in rocks; Eating mustang meat.*

Both downstream and upstream from location, the Expedition's scouts must have found the bluffs above the Rio Grande too high for another crossing, so it is no surprise that the following day the Expedition ride west, up the plateau above the river canyons. If Hays was still seeking a route suitable for a wagon road, his search was almost over.

Although SAM provided only a distance of 10 miles with no direction, their trail must have been close to what is now called "The Original Road" to the west-northwest, most likely an old Indian trail from Rattlesnake Canyon to Lozier Canyon. Travel along the Rio Grande would have been impossible since two large canyons (Rattlesnake and Ramsey) plus several smaller ones block any route along the river bluffs. This night, the Expedition camped at a waterhole in Lozier Canyon through which a major Indian trail led down to a Rio Grande crossing into Mexico.

Oct. 2, *To banks of Rio Grande, where we killed and ate a panther.*

The creek bed of Lozier Canyon with its broad white pathway of Lower Cretaceous limestone down the canyon to the river looks more like a major highway today than a creek bed. The distance in the canyon from near U.S. Highway 90, where waterholes were easily seen, down to the Rio Grande is almost exactly the same (6 miles) as SAM recorded, leaving little doubt about their route to the river. The "panther" (most likely a mountain lion) that they killed and ate was one of the few wild animals which provided food for the group on their section of the Trail.

Oct 3, Go out rocky creek and intersect a big trail and followed to the Rio Grande again at a great Indian crossing.

If a question existed about the location of the Expedition's campsite on October 3rd, SAM's entry answered that question because no other location fit his description of the day's travel. The group had to have ridden up Palma Canyon, a dry creek which enters Lozier Canyon from the west side just above the Rio Grande, toward the Dryden Plateau. From Palma Canyon they could have ridden west up one the creeks draining into Palma Canyon.

Once they were riding west up a creek, finding the major Indian trail down which they rode back to the Rio Grande would have been fairly easy. The trail had to have been through Bear Canyon to Mesquite Crossing, one of the major Indian crossings into Mexico, where they camped that night.

> *Oct 4th, Up river bottom - our course W.N.W. Camp at a spring - head of a creek - opposite to the bend (big bend of the Rio Grande) Mustang meat in great request.*

With no alternative route due to a series of high bluffs above the river, Hays and the Expedition rode up the Rio Grande, seeking another route out of the river farther upstream. SAM's "big bend of the Rio Grande" is caused by a large hill in Mexico around which the river flows and is on the south side of where Indian Creek meets the Rio Grande. The "head of a creek" must have referred to the Indian Creek confluence near which a spring was found for a campsite.

> *Oct 5th, Lookout Peak. In to the river; out again. Pass two Indian piles of stone. Camp at water hole in rock. Watering with pans, going say 5 W.N.W.*

The upriver course from the Indian Creek campsite is initially due south (the other side of SAM's "big bend") so the Expedition left the river to continue westward. The most likely exit was one of several small canyons which draining down to the river on the American side of the river bluff and this day's campsite clearly was not near the river because they had to "pan" a waterhole to get water. Based on the short distance ridden, i.e. "going say 5 W.N.W.", the "Lookout Peak" to which he referred is now called Loma Vista, the first of several isolated bluffs above the river that can fit the description of a lookout peak. However, Loma Vista is far enough above the hills and canyons emptying into the Rio Grande that Jack Hays and his scouts could easily see that the lands to the northwest opened up around the Dryden Plateau.

Previous historical references to the 1848 Pioneer Expedition led by Jack Hays have included his getting lost as he traveled west along the Rio Grande. After we personally re-explored those lands along the river, usually to photograph the major 1848 campsites, we could see, just as Jack Hays and the expedition members could have seen over 150 years before, that finding a route from Loma Vista to the southwest along the river appeared to be impossible due to the mountain Sierra Cuchilla La Chulita range. The result was that Jack Hays and his men were forced to seek another route on the American side of the river in order to Chihuahua. Although SAM's entry the following day doesn't describe how difficult the day's ride was, a major change to the northwest away from the river was required if the expedition was to reach Chihuahua.

However, what they saw across the river was a greater and unexpected obstacle blocking their travel to Chihuahua. A mountain range, Sierra Cuchilla La Chulita, rose from the plains in far northwestern Coahuilla with peaks up to 3,000 feet in elevation and extended from the Rio Grande southward to the Serrania del Burros forty miles away. What could not be seen behind the mountain range was the Mesa Juan Motas most of which is over 2,000 feet in elevation. Uplift of the mesa had turned the Rio Grande 90° from east to north below Burro Bluff and cut the final channel of the Rio Grande through the mesa up to its confluence with San Francisco Canyon. There the river flows eastward around the mesa toward Lozier Canyon and the Pecos River.

The mountain range, Sierra Cuchilla La Chulita, rises above the Mesa Juan Motas at its eastern border and marks the end of the Big Bend and the mesa. From the river the range extends to the south-southeast until a break separates it from a second range, Sierrra La Perdida. The two ranges end at the Serrania del Burros, creating an obstruction to southwest travel as far as the Hays Expedition could have seen. Although most histories of the expedition state that Jack Hays "got lost," the obvious reason for leaving the Rio Grande was that the view from "Lookout Peak" left them no choice but to seek a route to the northwest bypassing the Sierra Cuchilla range.

> *Oct 6th, Go about 15 W.N.W. & 5 S. of E. down creek to holes in rock. 1 1/2 mi from Rio Grande which here is running N. of E. Howard and Hays spy-glass.*

The distance and directions traveled this day were very confusing since riding south of east to reach a waterhole is impossible from Loma Vista and the east side of Sanderson Canyon. SAM's description of the campsite's being only 1 1/2 miles from where the Rio Grande runs north of east limits the location to only one possible site near the southeast end of Red House Canyon, west of Sanderson Canyon. Based on the mileages and directions, the Expedition must have crossed above several canyons, such as Jabalina and Taylor Canyons, before riding down Garcia Creek to cross Sanderson Canyon.

From Sanderson Canyon into which Lion Canyon flows barely above the Rio Grande, entry into the river was avoided and explains why the river was not mentioned by SAM. However, Lion Canyon is a short canyon with no source of water for the expedition. To find water that day, the expedition rode back southeast over a ridge and down Red House Canyon toward the river. Their campsite, described by SAM as being "holes in the rock," a mile and a half from the river, is also where the Rio Grande "runs" north of east. The only possible location fitting that day's campsite is in Red House Canyon where it ends at the river.

> Oct. 7th, Going W.N.W. Camp at edge of impassable ravine. Go back 1/2 mile to water horses. No food on hand; had scant breakfast. Here we begin to eat bear grass.

What SAM called an "impassable ravine" without water could not be determined from repeated analyses of several topographic maps, both 2D and 3D, of the trail up Red House Canyon. His description of the site, as several of SAM's daily entries had, failed to provide enough information to locate a campsite on the trail.

However, standing on the bluff overlooking a ravine of Isinglass Canyon about a half mile from that day's 1848 campsite, Jim and I felt that the expression, "impossible canyons," was more appropriate than SAM's "impassable ravine." All that could be seen to the south and southwest were limestone canyons and ravines, one after the other, with even taller mountains in the background, as far as one could see.

Over 150 years later the view was still discouraging since we saw no way to drive across those canyons despite our having a more than adequate supply of water and food supplies in our off-road vehicle. Finding that vast terrain, too rugged to be crossed by men with horses and mules, presented an extremely difficult, if not insoluble, problem to the Expedition's leader. However, Jack Hays had not lost his way because a route down the Rio Grande and back to San Antonio was possible. But no member of the

Expedition knew how to reach Chihuahua by riding down the "impassable ravine." Even more importantly, it confirmed that building a wagon road along the Rio Grande to Chihuahua or El Paso was clearly impossible.

> *Oct. 8th, Going W.N.W. in worst hills. Find a trail. Meet 3 Mezcaleros Indians (Apaches) take their back trail and enter the canyon of Mezcal Creek.*

The previous night's campsite had been on a ridge above an "impassable ravine" from which little could be seen other than one ravine or canyon after another to the south and southwest. On the morning of October 8th, the men rode west beside the ravine in what is now called Seminole Canyon. About a mile west of their campsite, the group came to a major Indian trail, now locally known as "Bullis Gap Road," up which they rode northward. Probably because their Delaware scouts found the Apaches, the Expedition leaders met with three Mescalero Apaches, a meeting described by Maverick's terse comment "Meet 3 Mezcalero Indians" (the word Apaches was an edit by his son-in-law), probably not far from where Bullis Gap Road intersects today's U.S. Highway 90. His entry was a brief and inadequate description of the meeting at best and describes almost nothing about the true significance of their situation at the time, i.e. the Expedition's members had no idea as to how they could reach Presidio del Norte. In his 1880 book,[36] John Henry Brown provides a more complete description of the meeting with the Mescalero Apaches based on his conversations with members of the expedition years later.

Meeting with Mescalero Apaches

"Thenceforward no man in the expedition knew the country. Having crossed the Pecos they found themselves in the rough, broken and unknown region lying between that stream and the Rio Grande. To men whose rations, as at this time, were about exhausted, it was a dismal succession of hill, vale and barranca. Lorenzo, the guide, failed to recognize the landmarks and became bewildered. In a day or two their supplies gave out. There was no game in the country, and, as many had been driven to do before, they resorted to their pack mules, the flesh of which was their only food for ten or twelve days. Fortunately a party of Mescalero Indians discovered them and, as Colonel Hays, from prudent motives with reference to Indians in that region, always had a white flag flying, came close enough to invite a talk, for which purpose three of their number met three of the Texians. After mutual explanations, easily understood on both sides through the Spanish language, and a liberal distribution of presents, with which the San Antonians were well supplied, they gave the party careful directions how to reach and cross the Rio Grande, and get to the Rancho San Carlos, on the Mexican side. Before reaching the river a doctor of the San Antonio party became deranged and wandered off. Five days after leaving the Mescaleros they arrived in San Carlos in a pitiable condition, where they procured a supply of food."

Author's Comments:

Brown's brief story about Hays expedition's meeting with the Mescalero Apaches confirms what Sam Maverick wrote about Hays and his group of explorers' encounter with the Mescaleros. The decision to leave the Rio Grande, after finding their way blocked by a mountain range to the southwest, to travel northwest was clearly a mistake. Despite the hardships suffered by the expedition's members during the next ten days before reaching San Carlos, the directions provided by the Mescalero Apaches were accurate and may have saved their lives. Of equal significance was Sam Maverick's description of Indian paintings in a canyon seen on the day following the Apache meeting, a critical piece of information in locating where the Expedition's leaders met with the Mescaleros. How we confirmed the location of the meeting is described in the following section.

> *Oct. 9th, Travel up same canyon. Determined to kill a mule, having nothing but mezcal bear grass to eat. Pictures on walls (of canyon). Splendid high walls. [Hieroglyphics or picture of ancient or Pueblo Indians probably as in N. Mex. & Ariz. E.H.T.].*

A major unanswered question about the Pioneer Expedition's trail since 1848 has been: where were the "Pictures on walls (of canyon)" and the "Splendid high walls" that SAM described in his entry of October 9, 1848? If the pictures and splendid high walls could be located, finding the final route of Sam Maverick's Trail to Presidio del Norte was possible. Since rock art ("Pictures on walls") can be found in several different locations in the region, the location of the rock art was useless information in finding the Expedition's final route to Chihuahua. However, more recent information about the region made locating the 1848 route to Chihuahua possible.

Starting with the use of topographic software on a computer, the writer backtracked from the three ridges of the Bullis Gap Range, unique structures (hogbacks) along the Expedition's trail to Dog Canyon, to the juncture of San Francisco Creek at the Rio Grande. From that junction down the Rio Grande to their previous camp (October 9th), the distance according to SAM's journal was twelve miles, placing the campsite at the mouth of Sanderson Canyon on the Rio Grande. When SAM's mileage was compared to the mileage shown in Louis Aulbach's river guide, The Lower Canyons of the Rio Grande,[37] the distance was exactly the same, twelve (12) miles. That made Sanderson Canyon the most likely site of the canyon with pictures on the walls as well as splendid high walls. Thus, the Expedition's route through the Big Bend could be backtracked to where they had climbed out of the Pecos River canyon if Sanderson Canyon was where pictures on the wall were seen by Sam Maverick.

Sometimes it's better to be lucky than to be good. A conversation with Billie Foster, a guide at Seminole Canyon State Park, provided the final, lucky clue. When the writer told Billie about the mileage calculations, indicating that the Indian paintings SAM had described might be in Sanderson Canyon, Billie said, "My husband (Billy) says there are Indian paintings in Sanderson Canyon." Consequently, an exploration of Sanderson Canyon to find the pictographs and photograph them, if they existed, was required.

We were also lucky in being able to arrange an exploration of Sanderson Canyon for wall paintings. While returning from a photo shoot, Jim and I stopped at the Terrell County (Texas) Courthouse and meet with Judge Dudley Harrison, owner of Harrison Ranch, the location of Sanderson Canyon. After describing our interest in Sanderson Canyon at the Courthouse, Dudley agreed not only to allow our hiking up the Canyon, but also agreed to assist us in our search for pictographs (rock art). Unfortunately, exploring and photographing desert canyons were far beyond this writer's ability, especially in the region's rugged terrain. So, an expert on Rock Art with experience hiking up river canyons was needed to accompany Jim Keller in searching for and photographing pictographs on the canyon walls if they were found. An email to Louis Aulbach and his enthusiastic response led to the following section by Louis about what they found and photographed in Sanderson Canyon.

The Discovery in Sanderson Canyon by Louis F. Aulbach

The Side Canyons of the Lower Rio Grande Canyons

There are many side canyons to the Rio Grande in the section of the Wild and Scenic River known as the Lower Canyons. Large drainages that have cut enormous side canyons enter the river from both sides, and explorations of the side canyons are one of the activities that make a trip through the remote wilderness of the Lower Canyons extra special.

However, the canyon walls which peak at over 900 feet above the river in the Bullis Fold recede substantially after one goes downstream of San Francisco Canyon, located near the Brewster County-Terrell County line. Add to that the fact that the usual river trip is nearly over and the take out is only a few miles ahead. As a result, very few river runners have explored the side canyons between San Francisco Canyon and the end of the trip at John's Marina at Dryden Crossing.

The chance to explore Sanderson Canyon was an opportunity that I could not let get away. so, when Dan Lane told me that he had arranged access with Dudley Harrison for November 7, 2004, I agreed to meet Dan and Jim Keller in Dryden that Sunday morning.

Dudley ("Judge Dud") Harrison, Owner of Sanderson Canyon

Sanderson Canyon is on the ranch of Dudley Harrison of Sanderson, who is almost as interesting as the hike down Sanderson Canyon itself. Dudley has been elected to nearly every office in Terrell County and has ranched in the area all his life. His father bought the current ranch about 1951 and had owned other land in the area since about 1925.

Dudley now has almost no animal stock since he liquidated his stock during the recent drought, and at age 75, he has no plans to rebuild his herd of goats and sheep. Mohair prices are way down, anyway.

After meeting in Dryden we followed Dudley to the ranch house which his father built in 1925 for his wife. The stone facade house sits on a bluff that overlooks a vast expanse of Texas to the west where the mountains near Marathon and the Big Bend can be seen. Dudley said that his father liked the rocky ground because he would not have to tend the yard, but his wife thought differently. She made him haul in loads of dirt so they could have a yard.

The Hike Up Sanderson Canyon

Dan, Jim Keller, the photographer, Dana Enos, a fellow wilderness canoer, and I packed into Dudley's Suburban and rode across the bumpy ranch roads to the Rio Grande at the cliff overlooking its junction with Sanderson Canyon. An old trail led down the cliff from the dilapidated old cabin on the top but was somewhat over grown, so reaching the ledges along the east side of the canyon required some brushwhacking.

At 10:00 a.m., we descended the rough trail down the rocky canyon walls to the brush and sand at the mouth of Sanderson Canyon. The water, which was still the chocolate shade of brown caused by the high quantity of sediment suspended in the water, had receded from earlier flooding enough that we were able to make our way up Sanderson Canyon by staying close to the rock base of the canyon wall. A few shrubs had grown over the trail, but by crawling low or breaking off the offending limbs, a clear path was made to a large rock ledge about twenty feet above the mud and water at the mouth of the creek.

Sanderson Canyon is relatively narrow and deeply cut with broad horizontal ledges on both sides. Hiking up the canyon there required working along the ledge on the east side, then down into the stream bed gravels, before climbing back up along the west side, often climbing boulders and clinging to footholds on high ledges. Limestone is very forgiving to the hiker and it offers a rough, non-slick surface. With good boots and a fair sense of balance, one can negotiate tight places that would seem impossible under other conditions. A couple of times, however, the traverse was so tight and challenging that I wondered if we should go back to the river.

The section that Dudley had suggested we explore was approximately four miles in length. Although Dudleyhad never been through the canyon himself, his father rode up from the canyon's mouth on a rock-climbing mule to chase his errant sheep and goats back up to pastures that were more accessible. His father's ability to ride up the canyon gave us hope that our route was feasible, but at times, it seemed questionable. So, we kept going and were able to negotiate each obstacle encountered. The side canyon walls were nearly straight up in this area, so there was no way out except upstream or back down again.

Dana and I kept our eyes out for signs of prehistoric sites since the main purpose of the hike was to locate the pictographs in the canyon mentioned in Sam Maverick's log. It was obvious, however, that there was little chance of finding any sites in the lower sections of the canyon. The lack of access from the rim above combined with the steepness of the walls and the well-washed canyon floor made inhabitable sites unlikely. Visually, though, the canyon was quite striking and oddly beautiful. The layer-cake formation of limestone was a ruddy brown stained with gray and black where the rain water had stained them gray with manganite. The rocks of this coloration extended down the canyon walls to the base of the canyon where the rocks were a lighter, whitish gray. This level at the floor of the canyon appeared bleached, however, the coloration may be due to the polishing of the rocks during times of turbulent flooding.

Looking back toward the river, the canyon was a long straight slot cut into the desert plateau. Ahead of us was a large tinaja bordered on both sides by huge white boulders. The ledge to the right pinched out, so we had to climb the boulders on the left and make our way up and around the pool below. The tinaja appeared to be several feet deep in places and the sides of the pool rose steadily to about twenty feet or so, preventing access out of the pool. Fortunately, there was only one treacherous spot along the left side. After considering the best route, we were able to use toe holds and finger grips to work around a narrow place along the cliff face. This was the only time in the whole trip that we had to assist each other by passing packs and gear ahead while the person concentrated on making the right step.

Once on the next ledge, the path was easier. A uniform layer of limestone created a high pour-off into the tinaja below, but the creek bed above was a football field size area of sand and gravel between the vertical walls on each side. A side canyon that entered from the right had fed these smaller streambed particles into Sanderson Canyon. Although we did not realize it at the time, this was Garcia Creek, the first significant side canyon we would encounter in our hike. We forged ahead and stopped for lunch in the shade of the next ledge about noon. It had taken us about two hours to make the first mile of our hike and we had seen nothing to indicate that there was any Indian activity in this section of the canyon.

After lunch, the hiking in the canyon became somewhat easier. The canyon floor was broader and more open. The ledges to each side were lower and less broken into boulders. We could move freely and quickly to the next pour-off and succeeding ledge. There was no pools of water so is was often faster to walk down the middle of the sandy bottom toward the head of the next level. Once there, we could climb the four or five feet to the next ledge. Eventually, the ledges became less prominent and we simply walked in the sand and gravel of the bed of the canyon. We were making good time, but the afternoon was becoming hot. A break in the shade was necessary at intervals so each of us could catch our breath.

The Discovery

Using two-way radios we made contact several times with Dan and Dudley who were driving along the lands above the canyon. However we became confused about where we were in the canyon and told Dan we were approaching Garcia Creek, an alternate exit site. After another hour or so, we came to a side canyon, thinking it was Garcia Creek. It was now about 3:00 p.m. and I was becoming concerned about our progress. We did not want to get caught in the canyon after dark, and at this time of year, the sun sets about 5:30 p.m. Dana downloaded the GPS location, only to find we had actually made it all the way up the canyon to our original exit point, some three miles above Garcia Creek. What we had thought was Garcia Creek was actually a side canyon that Dudley had shown us on our way to the river where he had indicated there was a horse trail down into the canyon and was the way that he and his crew could ride into Sanderson Canyon.

Since our rendezvous was to be at 4:00 p.m. and we were still interested in solving the question of the pictographs. I surveyed the streambed ahead where the canyon walls appeared to be undercut, so Jim and I continued up the canyon to look for the pictographs while Dana climbed out of the canyon to try and contact Dan and Dudley. About a quarter of a mile upstream we found a shelter with a lot of black smoke and some faint markings below that may have been pictographs. After more scouting around, I noticed an alcove-type shelter directly across from the smoke-blackened shelter with markings that looked like pictograph colorings. It was not exactly what I was expecting, but the pictograph might have been what had been written about. The large amount of smoke on the overhang suggested that this shelter had been used repeatedly for years. The sand in the canyon had filled in much of the overhang and perhaps had covered other evidence of prehistoric occupation and pictographs.

The location of the shelter in the vicinity of the side canyon drainage that provided easy access into the canyon seemed appropriate. A slope of the canyon on the opposite side was gentle enough to provide a route of egress for travelers crossing Sanderson Canyon. From our exploration of the lower sections of the canyon, this was the first place above the Rio Grande where horsemen could travel from east to west across the canyon. The fact that there are ranch roads on the plateau at this point on both sides of the canyon seems to verify that fact.

A Night-Time Reminder

Hiking an additional quarter mile or so up the canyon didn't locate another site of human occupation, so I returned to our exit point while Jim finished taking photos of the smoky shelter and the pictograph alcove. When I got back to where Dana was waiting on the canyon rim, Dudley's car could be seen, coming up the road. In a few minutes, Jim came out of the canyon and we headed back to the ranch house just in time to see a spectacular sunset from Dudley's back yard. Then, once we'd re-packed our gear, Dan and Jim headed east, back to San Antonio, while Dana and I turned west to Sanderson and hamburgers at the T & C gas station. From there we drove to the Big Bend, arriving at the Hannold Draw campsite about 9:30 p.m., where we camped for the night after a long and successful day.

As I lay dreaming of Sanderson Canyon in the early hours of morning, I thought I heard coyotes howling twice during the night. At dawn, I awoke to find their footprints in the sand and realized that the coyotes had danced alongside my cot twice during the night, not five feet from where I had been sleeping. It reminded me of something I already knew. The River Canyon Country and the Big Bend of Texas are still wild and largely untamed by the modern world, but one has to get off the highway to discover what's there.

Author's Comments:

Finding a blackened roof with pictographs on both sides of Sanderson Canyon supports the geographic and topographic data which indicate that the

1848 Expedition traveled by the canyon on their way back to the Rio Grande and Rancho San Carlos. Although the ground below the blackened roof has not been excavated seeking mortar holes for cooking by early inhabitants, who most likely were nomadic Indian tribes, the presence of a midden on the bluff above, a nearby spring and a break in the canyon walls where horses could cross the canyon above the pictographs were additional evidence that Sanderson Canyon had been part of an ancient Indian trail used not only by the Mescalero Apaches but by prehistoric inhabitants as well.

The hike up the canyon by Louis, Dana and Jim also proved that the 1848 Expedition could not have ridden through the canyon because a drop-off, tinaja and the rocky channel block travel by horse or mule up or down the canyon. Since the most easily observed section of the ancient site was on the western side, the 1848 Expedition's route probably rode above the eastern side of Sanderson Canyon, much the same route as we drove down to the Rio Grande where the canyon's exploration began. A trail on the Mexico side leading upstream to San Francisco Canyon was easily visible from the bluff above Sanderson Canyon.

Although a very long day ended with a long and tiring drive back to San Antonio, Jim and I left Harrison Ranch more than pleased about having found the missing pictograph site on the 1848 Expedition's route to San Carlos that Sam Maverick had described in his journal. Despite the complicated preparation required, the photographs of Sanderson Canyon are special enough to have justified a long and difficult hike through Sanderson Canyon. And, with no coyotes howling to awaken us during the night, we both slept very soundly after an exhausting return home.

A Band of Texans Explores the Big Bend

The boundary of the Big Bend is the Rio Grande from its confluence with the Rio Conchos at La Junta de los Rios downstream to its eastward turn at San Francisco Canyon, a direct distance of approximately 140 miles. From north to south, that is, from the Davis Mountains south to Mariscal Mountain in Big Bend National Park, the distance is about the same as that east-to west, forming a complex and rugged diamond-shaped territory. Within that territory are the spectacular geological structures of Big Bend National Park and unique flora and fauna due to its location in the North Chihuahuan desert. The origin of the Big Bend is extremely complex to define due to repeated periods of tectonic activity in the region that have occurred over hundreds of millions of years.[38]

During the early Paleozoic Era, the North American continent separated from a massive land mass, allowing for the deposition of eroded materials from the Precambrian continent. Then, during the late Paleozoic, the continents collided again to form Panagea. During that period of activity, a high mountain range composed of Paleozoic debris was produced, stretching from Texas across the United States and northern Europe. However, during the early Mezozoic Era tectonic activity again broke Panagea apart into what would become today's continents with an inland sea spread across North America.

By the late Mezozoic Era, the inland sea covered the western United States from the Arctic Sea down through South America. During the Cretaceous Period, massive amounts of limestone and other aquatic minerals were deposited thousands of feet deep across Texas. Then, as North America separated from Europe to form the Atlantic Ocean, the high Palezoic mountain range (Ouachita Trend) was compressed southwestward where it collided with formation of the Rocky Mountains (Laramide Orogeny) to create the Big Bend.

During the Cenozoic Era, alternating periods of compression and relaxation opened fissures where the collision occurred. Those changes produced what was the most violent period of volcanic activity in United States history with at least five major calderas in the Big Bend region. Today's Big Bend National Park is located in the southeastern margin of the volcanism. The entire area of volcanic eruptions was covered by ash expelled from the volcanoes that would require millions of years to be washed and blown away. The mountains and canyons created during formation of the Big Bend had a direct effect upon the 1848 Pioneer Expedition by the formation of mountains and canyons blocking their way to Chihuahua.

One of the first obstacles that the expedition was the increase in elevation from the Rio Grande up to Maravillas Creek in the Marathon Basin of almost 1500 feet. However, if the Expedition had tried to continue up San Francisco Creek to its origin, the increase would have been even greater. In the 75 miles from its origin in the Marathon Basin, San Francisco Creek drops 3000 feet in elevation to join the Rio Grande. The changes in the Lower Canyons of the Rio Grande at San Francisco Creek have been frozen in time since massive river flooding is relatively rare and downcutting of the near-vertical canyons over millions of years ago remained much the same in 1848. So, by the time the Pioneer Expedition arrived at San Francisco

Canyon, the canyons had been cut so deeply in the Lower Canyons that further travel along the Rio Grande was no longer possible.

> *Oct. 10th, Kill mule and eat our breakfast. Travel up same canyon. Found abundance of fine tunas. Camp at head of the Mezcal canyon - sick of tunas. Our mule meat very poor and tough. R.A. Howard's bear grass soup. Here we are at the highest, with horizontal strip of limestone. Going W.N.W.*

As the Expedition rode up the Rio Grande to San Francisco Canyon, SAM noted a change in the river bluffs to the "highest mountains, with limestone zone." In the twelve miles from Sanderson to San Francisco Canyon, the bluffs above the river on the American side increase from 1400 feet to over 2000 feet in elevation while the river bottom rises less than fifty feet. Sam Maverick's entry for October 10, 1848 described the change in elevation: "Here we are at the highest mountains, with horizontal strip of limestone." The bluffs, which had been only one hundred and fifty feet above the river at Sanderson Canyon, are six to seven hundred feet above the Rio Grande/San Francisco Canyon junction on the American side.

The changes on the Mexican side of the river were more important since that was how the Mescaleros had bypassed the obstruction caused by the Sierra Cuchilla La Chulita mountain range and the Mesa Juan Motas. Twelve miles south of San Francisco Canyon, Mesa Juan Motas is almost 2,000 feet above the the Rio Grande river and continues up to the river's junction with San Francisco Canyon. The mesa is composed of relatively uniform Cretaceous limestone and turns the Rio Grande 90° northward with no visible faulting along its northward course to its junction with San Francisco Canyon. Once past that junction, the Rio Grande flows eastward around the mesa and the Sierra Cuchilla to join the Pecos River many miles away. Thus, the Big Bend of Texas ends at the junction of the Rio Grande and meets San Francisco Canyon where travel up the river was prevented by the lack of a trail and sharply rising bluffs.

The Sierra Cuchilla range and its extension to the south-southeast, La Sierra Perdida, are "fissure volcanoes" created when the tectonic compression from the east that raised the Mesa Juan Motas relaxed. The release of pressure opened a fissure along the east side of the mesa, allowing the eruption of magma up through the fissure to create the volcanoes that extend twenty-five miles from the Rio Grande SSE to the Serrania del Burros. The presence of a "hoodoo" (welded ash) in Taylor canyon on Harrison Ranch only five miles across the river from Sierra Cuchilla La Chulita is powerful evidence that the volcanic eruption was close by. The linear extension of a blade-like volcanic mountain ranges is also a characteristic of fissure volcanos and if their age was determined, then the time of the tectonic event that lifted up Mesa Juan Motas might be established.[34, p. 39]

However, the Expedition faced more serious problems than the height of the "mountains" or canyons, that is, the need to find food for the expedition's members and their animals. The "fine tunas," the ripe fruit of cacti, are better than nothing to eat, but not adequate nutrition for days. "R.A. Howard's bear grass soup" sounds even less appealing, so having to kill a pack mule, despite its tough meat, leaves little doubt about the group's nearing starvation. What Sam Maverick and the expedition's members didn't know was that they had reached the point in the Rio Grande's course where the river ends as a boundary of the Big Bend. Their food supply would have to be found somewhere along the trail described by the Mescaleros.

> *Oct 11th, Travel up 1 1/2 miles - Come to big trail going S. of W. Camp on creek which runs W.S.W. Lost 8 horses and mules stolen by Indians, who had been riding two horses and had [a] dog.*

The big trail going S. of W. after leaving the river was up San Francisco Creek since the high bluffs forced them to follow the advice of the Mescaleros. Above San Francisco Canyon, the creek bed is quite tortuous and the trail had risen almost 1,000 feet, based on SAM's mileage, by the time they made camp in Barrel Canyon. That canyon runs W.S.W. from San Francisco Creek as SAM wrote and is also below the first hogbacks of the Bullis Gap Range.

No comment was made about where the Indians stole the horses and mules, but the presence of a dog was apparently significant despite SAM's not providing an explanation.

> *Oct 12th, Down same creek and over broadplain for 10 miles. Cross 3 ridges running S.E. We going S. Camp at spring dug out by Indians in salt plain. Dr. Wahm crazy.*

Of SAM's entries in his journal describing the exploration, the entry for October 12th provided important information for connecting the section between Sanderson Canyon and Dog Canyon. Although the landforms they passed were not recorded in proper sequence by SAM, three of the features he mentioned were critical to making the connection between Trail segments. The most important was his reference to "3 ridges running S.E.," which are three ridges unique to this area in the eastern Big Bend. By location, those ridges could only be what is now called the Bullis Gap Range, which geologically are three "hogbacks" of the type found in arid or semi-arid regions.[33] Formed by harder rock eroding more slowly than softer rock in the formation, the southwest sides of the ridges gradually were worn down into small canyons, draining southeast toward the Rio Grande.

The "broadplain for 10 miles" describes a special feature, that is, the plain from the eastern edge of the Maravillas Creek basin near Beef Canyon to the "spring" by Dove Mountain. Shorter plains in the area would have required a longer route to reach the spring because any route east of Barrel Canyon is blocked either by hogbacks or the Rio Grande.

The "spring dug out by Indians" was the final feature that confirmed the location of the westward section of Sam Maverick's Trail. The Dove Mountain tinaja is south of Dove Mountain at the edge of a broad plain. Although Indians often dug in the earth for shallow sources of water, the Dove Mountain tinaja with its stable level of water is the most likely campsite for October 12th and mileage from the eastern edge of the basin to the tinaja is the best fit for this days campsite. Finding a good source of water on the 12th was fortunate since the next day's ride, besides being both long and arduous, proved to be especially hard on their horses.

An interesting and significant entry by SAM was that a member of the Expedition (Doctor Wahm) was "crazy" that day. Considering the obstacles that the expedition had faced by this day, the real surprise is that no Expedition member hadn't already "gone crazy."

> Oct. 13th, Travel 20 S.S.E. and 10 S.S.W. breaking down 10 or 15 horses trying to reach water. Camp late at night on stony hill without water.

The 1848 Pioneer Expedition left Dove Mountain tinaja and rode west to Dog Canyon as described by Maverick. This day, October 13, 1848, the

Texan explorers, by crossing the Maravillas Creek basin and entering what is now Big Bend National Park by riding through Dog Canyon, were the first Americans to explore this unique site in North America where "all hell broke loose" as repeated collisions and separations split open the earth's crust, exploding magma and ash to cover the Big Bend with layers of lava and welded ash ("ignimbrites"). At least five major volcanic calderas were involved in this process, creating too many landforms in the National Park to describe.

However, the October 13th entry in SAM's journal includes a major error or exclusion as to the direction of travel by the Expedition this day. A ride of 20 miles S.S.E. and S.S.W. from the tinaja was impossible because only mountains, river canyons and the Rio Grande can be found in that direction. The Expedition had to have ridden W.S.W to reach Dog Canyon if they were to cross the Rio Grande by October 15th. How or why the correct direction (W.S.W.) and distance were deleted in SAM's original journal makes little difference because the Expedition members had to ride almost due west from the tinaja to reach Dog Canyon. If the W.S.W. direction with mileage had been included, then the Trail into what is now Big Bend National Park could have been found long ago.

Adding the deleted west-southwest direction, the group rode from the Dove Mountain tinaja to Maravillas Creek, passing through a ridge, then west along the creek up to the east entrance of Dog Canyon. Measured on a computer's topographic map, the distance is almost exactly 20 miles. After riding through the canyon in or by Nine Point Draw, the group traveled another ten miles S.S.E. past Dagger Mountain, then S.S.W. to camp on a ridge from Dog Canyon.

Several ridges can be found south of Dog Canyon, but the mileage to the campsite fits best with a location at the east end of the ridge between Dagger Flats and Rosillos Mountain. This ridge is large enough to separate water falling north of the ridge, forcing the water to drain northward up to Nine Point Draw at Dog Canyon. Since we re-explored this area during a driving rainstorm, our photographs of the waterflow during the storm confirmed that rain falling north of the ridge flows down through Dog Canyon into Maravillas Creek. Although difficult to see in the photograph because of the rainstorm, the ridge separates the flat terrain of north end from the south side (Tornillo Flat) and the rugged topography south of the ridge created by volcanic activity over millions of years.

> *Oct 14th, 12 miles to water. Camp. Wait for our benighted men. Dr. Wahm rode off in a fury last night. Suppose he is lost. Send back home for lame and crazy.*

Because of the a massive rainstorm, Tornillo Flat, one of the driest areas in the Big Bend National Park, is covered with floodwaters overflowing the banks of Tornillo Creek. Desert plants, such as ocotillos, are easily recognized in the foreground, although their lack of flowers suggests that the current rainfall had not been preceded by an earlier storm. The hills and mountains in the background are also obscured by the rain, making their identification difficult. Obviously we photographed Tornillo Flat under much different conditions than what SAM described as "a stony hill without water."

After camping on the ridge, the Expedition's trail down Tornillo Creek finally led them to a waterhole or a spring on the 14th. Since a large number of springs can still be found along Tornillo Creek above the Rio Grande, including hot springs at the river, the specific source of "water" SAM mentioned could not be determined since "12 miles" fits the locations of several springs in or near the creek. This campsite was their last in the United States since the following day they rode down to the Rio Grande and crossed at a river ford to camp in Mexico.

Unfortunately, their progress was slowed when "Dr. Wahm rode off in a fury last night," indicating that the doctor deserted the expedition. Maverick's plan for Doctor Wahm, that is, to "Send back home for lame and crazy," suggests that Sam Maverick was also affected by the mental and physical conditions created during a more difficult exploration than had been expected. Even in the 21st Century, sending a "lame and crazy" person back to San Antonio from the south end of Big Bend National Park is almost impossible except by air. How Maverick planned to send Doctor Wahm back to San Antonio in 1848 is hard to imagine.

> *Oct 15th, Go 1 1/2 miles down dry creek to ford two or three hundred varas above mouth of said creek. Camp south west side of Rio Grande. Wait for men gone for Wahm. Rio Grande here runs East.*

The exact location of this day's campsite could not be determined initially because several creeks are located in the area. Once Tornillo Creek was confirmed as the "dry creek" on which the October 14th campsite was made, the first location in Mexico was easily determined since the Rio Grande only flows eastward for a short distance near its junction with Tornillo Creek. To the east, the rive passes through Hot Springs Canyon and the course upstream of the Rio Grande turns sharply to the south-southeast and Sierra San Vicente. This campsite was also east of the big Comanche Road crossing the river into Mexico, probably because the Mescaleros could reduce their chances of having contact with the Comanches.

Through Mexico to La Junta de los Rios

After leaving the Tornillos Creek junction at the Rio Grande, the westward exploration around the Big Bend continued southward in Mexico on "big Comanche Road (of twenty trails)," probably through Sierra San Vicente which blocks a direct route west to San Carlos along the Rio Grande. The directions from the Mescaleros about the route to San Carlos must have included directions about the ruins of Presidio San Vicente, since from those ruins, their travels from their first Rio Grande campsite to Fort Leaton should have been much easier. A road had been built by the Spaniards in the 18th Century between Presidio San Vicente and Presidio San Carlos to Presidio del Norte as part of their "northern line of defense." SAM's entries on October 16th about a "Hilly road" and on October 20, 1848 "Camp in road on Cr." support the existence of such a road on the Mexican side of the river even though Presidio San Vicente had been in ruins for decades. The mileages and directions recorded by SAM, as well as his comments about San Vicente and San Carlos, indicate that despite the lack of topographic confirmation, the Pioneer Expedition's route in Mexico was close to the Rio Grande and over the original road between the old Spanish presidios. However, the route for the Trail in Mexico is at best an estimate since modern topographic data on the Mexican side of the border were not available for confirmation and older maps of the region showed that the names and locations on the maps varied significantly from one era to the next.

> Oct 16th Fitzgerald came late last night; two others in the morning. They found but did not secure and finally lost the unhappy crazy man in the

> black ravines. We go S.S.W. on big Comanche Road (of twenty trails) to Durango etc. Volcanic formation as on east side of Rio Grande. San Vicente is two or three Lgs. below ford. Hilly road. Camp at spring (in Mexico).

Maverick's entry for the 16th includes several interesting observations. The first was that Doctor Wahm had escaped from the men trying to bring him back to the Expedition. As the members would learn long after their return to San Antonio, the doctor managed to survive his escape and ultimately returned home, primarily because of his capture by a friendly Indian tribe. The privations Wahm and the other members of the Expedition had suffered up to this time were more than enough to have driven a man crazy.

The second of SAM's comments states that they rode S.S.W. down the "big Comanche road ("of twenty trails"), which was along the Rio Grande on a route by the ruins of Presidio San Vicente, approximately two or three miles, not "two or three leagues," from the ford. After reaching Sierra San Vicente, the trail turned down the east side of the Sierra, probably on an old Spanish road SAM referred to as a "Hilly road." A spring, which was on the old road from Presidio San Vicente to Presidio San Carlos, must have been the night's campsite.

His third comment about finding volcanic formations on both sides of the Rio Grande is still true today. What SAM could not have known was that for the next two to three weeks the Expedition would be riding on or living in a region created by intense volcanic activity. His limited description of what they saw in this area is unfortunate since so little is known about what was there in 1848 and volcanic activity is responsible for most of the difficult terrain.

The original plan for re-exploring and photographing Sam Maverick's Trail around the Big Bend had been to travel to the states of Coahuila and Chihuahua, Mexico, but a political reality intervened. Following the September 11th, 2001 World Trade Center disaster in New York City, many border crossings between Texas and Mexico were in effect closed down and crossing into Mexico became progressively more difficult. The closest legal crossings of the Texas-Mexico border to the Trail were at Presidio/Ojinaja and Del Rio/Cuidad Acuna, which are hundreds of miles apart and on roads over difficult terrain. Unexpectedly, getting into and out of Mexico to find the 1848 Expedition's route became a complex problem. In addition, despite the availability of excellent topographic maps and computer software for the American side of the Rio Grande, topographic data of equivalent accuracy could not be found for the Mexican side despite contacting multiple sources. The consequence was that SAM's mileage and directions for the Mexican section of the Trail could not be used to find that part of the Trail along the Rio Grande, so historical information with extrapolation were used to locate the Expedition's approximate route.

> *Oct 17th Quit the Comanche road. Travel W. and W.N.W. & N.W. Camp on branch and here kill the 4th pack mule.*

Their exit from the Comanche road was most likely on the "presidio road" built by the Spanish government from Presidio San Vicente to Presidio San Carlos. The last of their food supply had been consumed several days before and no wild game had been killed on the trail through the Big Bend. Since the expedition's members hadn't eaten in days, killing a fourth pack mule was required in order to provide at least minimal nourishment.

> *Oct. 18th N.W. 6 m. W. 4 m. up irrigable creek of the San Carlos settlement. Camp on hill opposite San Carlos.*

> *Oct. 19th In camp - recruiting on bread and milk.*

SAM's description of San Carlos being located "up an irrigable creek" fits the site to which the Spaniard, Hugo Oconor, had moved the presidio of Cerro Gordo from a location closer to the Rio Grande. But a new Rancho San Carlos may have been on Arroyo San Carlos with water and land suitable for farming. When Hays arrived there with the Pioneer Expedition, the small settlement was extremely poor with a very limited supply of food available, even for its own people. Despite the community's poverty, bread and milk, the first real food they had eaten in twelve days, were provided for the starving explorers. The food from San Carlos and a day's rest assured that the westward exploration to Chihuahua would be completed. Hays, Highsmith, Maverick, Howard and every member of the Pioneer Expedition owed a special debt to the people of San Carlos who gave or sold them enough bread and milk to reach Fort Leaton.

> Oct. 20th Camp in road on Cr. N.W.

Rested and fed, they again traveled toward Presdio del Norte, camping this night near a creek on the road. Based on its distance from Fort Leaton, the road was by a stream near Colorado Canyon, either where Panther Creek enters the Rio Grande or below Santanna Mesa. Upstream from this site, floodplain of La Junta de los Rios spreads out along the Rio Grande from its eastern edge. Finding a place to camp on the road, where a relatively level plain exists, is no surprise.

> Oct. 21st Rainy & muddy. Camp at hole.

This day, the Pioneer Expedition rode across the broad flood plain of La Junta, leaving behind the rough, high and dry region they had just found along the Rio Grande. The small community of El Mulato, Chihuahua is now located near where they probably camped, although no one lived there in 1848. But, within a few years, a small town was founded by people of African ancestry whose origin has been debated. The most common explanation had been that they were runaway slaves or deserters from the U.S. Army. However, thousands of slaves were brought from Africa to Mexico to work in silver mines, after which they were said to have intermingled with the native Indian population. Since Chihuahua had several silver mines, slaves brought there to work the mines are the most likely source, although all three sources may have contributed to the founding of El Mulato. But in 1848, the only significance this camp had was that it was their last campsite in Mexico before re-crossing the Rio Grande to reach Fort Leaton.

> Oct. 22nd Sunday. Recross Rio Grande near Leaton and camp about 1 m. east of Ft. Leaton, which is called 5 miles east of Presidio del Norte, making us 6 or 7 E. of Presidio del Norte.
> 57th day - No food for 12 days before reaching San Carlos. 418 (miles) to where we left the Pecos and 329 to P. del Norte = 747 (miles).

The Expedition's westward exploration, which had started at Las Moras Springs, had finally reached Chihuahua despite their camping across the Rio Grande at the fort. The exploration had been far more difficult and taken longer than anyone could have predicted before their departure, but had been safely completed when they crossed the river at Fort Leaton, except for Doctor Wahm's riding off into the wilds of the Big Bend.

Despite their arrival at the fort, a new and different problem had to be dealt with by Hays, Highsmith and the other leaders , i.e. should the Pioneer Expedition continue on to El Paso or return to San Antonio and Castell? During the several days of recovery at Fort Leaton, while the members rested and the Expedition was re-supplied, preparations were made to either ride on to El Paso or to search for an east-west route suitable for a wagon road.

Fort Leaton

Originally constructed as a *fortin*, or small fort, by Captain Jose Ignacio Ronquillo, the commander of Presidio del Norte, as an outpost to protect farmers on the Rio Grande downstream from the presidio,[40] the property was acquired by an American, Ben Leaton, after the Treaty of Guadalupe Hidalgo through a series of slightly, if not completely, illegal transactions through the Mexican authorities in Presidio del Norte. After securing control of the old fortin, Leaton both expanded and fortified what had been a small military post into a safe residence for both his family and his associates. Ben Leaton's major activity as owner of the fort was as a trader with residents of both sides of the Rio Grande, including residents of Presidio, Anglo travelers and various Indian tribes, especially the Mescalero Apaches. However, our interest in Fort Leaton and its owner, Ben Leaton, is limited to their significant role in supporting the first two explorations of the Texas-Mexico border, the 1848 Pioneer (Hays) Expedition and the 1849 Whiting-Smith Reconnaissance.

After managing to survive its exploration through the Big Bend by obtaining food at Rancho San Carlos, the first Anglo-American expedition to arrive at Fort Leaton was the 1848 Pioneer Expedition led by Jack Hays with forty-nine armed men and ten Delaware Indians. Their route to Fort Leaton, based on Sam Maverick's entries, was probably over the Spanish road built between the presidios which had long been abandoned. Based on the mileage record, the expedition did not stop at Presidio del Norte before crossing the Rio Grande to camp at Fort Leaton on the American side. One mile east of the fort, the expedition camped in an old adobe house, most likely one of the original farmer's home protected by Captain Ronquillo's original *fortin*, where they stayed until fully prepared for a return to San Antonio.

Ben Leaton, who had rebuilt the old fort to serve as a trading post, must have assisted Hays and the expedition's leaders in preparing for their return. Sam Maverick's comments are very brief about their stay at Fort Leaton, in effect, little more than a description of the supplies and their costs that had been purchased for their travels. Since Leaton had moved to the American side with his family from Chihuahua City in early 1848, the Expedition's new supplies probably had been brought to the fort from Chihuahua, an expensive and dangerous undertaking. However, after camping at the fort and being re-supplied with Ben Leaton's help, the Pioneer Expedition left from Presidio del Norte on October 31st for San Antonio. Their route was northeast to Alamitos Creek, only two miles east of Fort Leaton, then up what would become the major Chihuahua trail between San Antonio and the treasures of Chihuahua. Swift's comment in his book about the Chihuahua Trails[26] leaves little doubt about both the expedition's return route and its significance: "This is important, for it does establish that Hays was the first Anglo-American, in scouting out the Alamitos Creek route, to use it as a link in the ultimately feasible road to the Gulf Coast." However, despite that success, the 1848 Pioneer Expedition left Fort Leaton without completing its exploration of the Texas-Mexico border from La Junta de los Rios to El Paso del Norte, primarily because the expedition to Chihuahua had already required too much time. The remaining section of the border would not be explored until the 1849 Whiting-Smith reconnaissance, with the assistance of several members of the 1848 expedition, explored the Rio Grande above La Junta. The success of the second exploration also depended upon the safety and resources that Fort Leaton and Ben Leaton could provide.

Fortunately, Whiting and Smith, the leaders of the second expedition, knew before leaving San Antonio that because of the Pecos River, a route along the Rio Grande to La Junta was not adequate for construction of a road to Chihuahua or El Paso del Norte. Consequently, they chose a more northern route for travel to Presidio del Norte as suggested by Jack Hays, a recommendation which proved to be a mixed blessing. The abundant waterholes west of the San Saba River that Hays described had dried up, but the expedition's animals and humans survived long enough to reach Live Oak Creek. From there, except for riding up the west side of the Pecos,

Whiting-Smith followed the Hays route to Horsehead Crossing and up to Comanche Springs.

Dick Howard must have remembered the "two days and four hours without water" noted by Maverick, so the second exploration's route west was close to that of today's Interstate Highway 10 to San Solomon's Springs at Balmorrhea. Unfortunately, despite the many sources of water along the route, they caught the attention of a large Apache raiding party returning from Mexico. Due to a clever ruse by Whiting, they escaped the Apaches by riding away from their "Painted Trees" camp at night to a more secure campsite near a stack of volcanic boulders west of the future site of Fort Davis.

Whiting's description of his route south to Fort Leaton created confusion about his route to reach the fort. Although he claimed to have ridden down Cibolo Creek, the mileage he recorded would have taken the expedition no farther than the northwest side of today's Marfa, Texas where he camped on what was a tributary of Alamitos Creek. The structures Whiting described on his route down the creek can still be seen in the valley of Alamitos Creek and their intersection with the Hays route up the creek fits where San Jacinto Creek enters Alamitos Creek. If there is any doubt of which creek he followed and where Fort Leaton was located, Whiting's entry about looking down on the fort less than a mile away with smoke from Presidio del Norte visible in the distance establishes that he had to be on the ridge which still separates Fort Leaton from Alamitos Creek. Ben Leaton welcomed Whiting upon his arrival and made a special effort to provide food and a campsite for the expedition's members.

Leaton was even more supportive of the Whiting-Smith's exploration up the Rio Grande than for the Hays group return to San Antonio. Besides preparing a limited supply of food (dried beef, pinole and corn meal) for their trip, he also assisted in obtaining new animals to replace those which were no longer fit for the expedition's travels. Because of the dangers they faced up the Rio Grande, Ben Leaton even sent two of his associates to El Paso with the expedition and rode up the river during the first day.

In addition, Leaton took Whiting, Smith, Howard and Delacy to meet the commandant of Presidio del Norte, Don Guillermo Ortiz, who welcomed them with a Mexican dinner. Whiting's observation of the small community and its presidio was that it was a "miserable, Indian-blighted place." The town was relatively immune from Indian depredations because its inhabitants had already been stripped of what was worth stealing. Even the very rich mines on both sides of the river had been abandoned because the miners had been driven off by Indians.

Before his exploration up the Rio Grande above La Junta de los Rios, Lieutenant Whiting inspected the Fort Leaton and made the following observations about the location and future value of fortin:[41] "Fort Leaton will become an important site to the United States in view of the treaty stipulation and the Indian aggressions. It will make a convenient post, or depot, and refuge for the roving camps of dragoons which must be placed upon the great warpaths. Presidio is at the western part of the Rio Grande where most of these passes into Mexico exist. It is in convenient striking distance of the upper passes of the Apache. With a proper and efficient system of mounted troops, heavy blows will at one day or other be struck upon the Comanche from this post. It will also become the customhouse for the Chihuahua trade, destined to pass, henceforth, if I mistake not, not by Santa Fe, but from New Orleans and the southern states."

With a location adjacent to Alamitos Creek and the Chihuahua Trail to San Antonio, Fort Leaton proved to be an excellent site for the trading activities of Leaton and his associates. He even traveled to San Antonio and Indianola, the Gulf Coast port, during his trading days. However, as Morgenthaler has written,[42] Leaton title to the fort had never been legally re-established, including the role of Juana Pedraza, his mistress of may years and mother of his children. While in San Antonio during the summer of 1851 with his teamster, Ed Hall, to establish his ownership, Ben Leaton suddenly died and ownership of his estate became a major problem. Part of the problem was solved when Pedraza married Ed Hall, Leaton's former employee, and as Leaton's "widow" was entitled to the homestead under Texas law. However, as Morgenthaler noted,[42] "Less than five years after Ben Leaton cut a swath through the valley his fortin stood empty. Juana Pedraza, now married to Leaton's former teamster Ed Hall, was unwilling to venture back into the difficulty and danger of La Junta,..."

Fort Leaton would never have the military importance that Whiting envisioned in his diary, primarily because of Whiting and Smith's own findings during their return for El Paso del Norte. A more direct route through the Davis Mountains and the Devils River with adequate water for men and their animals bypassed the need for travel down Alamitos Creek. La Junta is still an active area today and remains the only legal port of entry into Mexico between El Paso and Del Rio. Today, tourist centers, not commercial trading, are the major economic activities where Fort Leaton still stands as a reminder of the earliest frontier days in the State of Texas.

5

RETURN EAST TO HOME / ALAMITOS CREEK AND PECOS RIVER VALLEY

Presidio del Norte to Horsehead Crossing

First described by Cabeza de Vaca as being an area inhabited by tall Indians wearing cotton clothes and living in well-built homes, La Junta de los Rios is the name for the large floodplain where the Rio Concho flows from Mexico into the Rio Grande. Now the location of the "twin cities" of Presidio, Texas and Ojinaja, Chihuahua, the region is one of the oldest, continuously cultivated regions in North America dating back to at least 1500 B.C. La Junta's confluence of two major rivers, its long history of human habitation, and central geographic location are the reasons why La Junta has long been a center of human civilization as well as many different trails for centuries before the first Spaniards arrived there.[43]

Based on what Cabeza de Vaca had written, a Franciscan lay brother, Augustin Rodriguez, and two Franciscan brothers, protected by eight Spanish soldiers, traveled down the Rio Concho to La Junta de los Rios in 1581.[44] From there, the explorers traveled up the Rio Grande to El Paso del Norte (now Cuidad Juarez, Chihuahua), before continuing up the river to Puaray, New Mexico between Albuquerque and Santa Fe where the Franciscans planned to start a mission for the local Indians. Unfortunately, following the soldiers' departure back to Mexico, the Franciscan brothers were massacred by the Indians they had planned to convert to Christianity. The rescue expedition in 1582–1583 was too late to save the martyred missionaries, but their exploration along the Rio Grande significantly affected the futures of Chihuahua, New Mexico and western Texas. The best evidence of their success is the road from La Junta de los Rios up the Rio Grande to El Paso del Norte which can still be traveled to this day.

Although a more direct route from Chihuahua City to El Paso del Norte had been built by the Spaniards before the Pioneer Expedition's arrival in 1848, the Franciscans' exploration along the Rio Grande from La Junta to El Paso proved to be of great value to Jack Hays in reaching a decision about continuing to explore up to El Paso. First, with an established road along the river from La Junta to El Paso del Norte, the location of the Texas-Mexico border upstream from Presidio del Norte was already known and few Indians lived there. Second, extending the Pioneer Expedition's exploration beyond Presidio del Norte to El Paso del Norte was of limited economic benefit because Chihuahua was the important destination for a wagon road in 1848, primarily to divert shipments of silver and other products to San Antonio and the Gulf. Third, and probably the most important, the Expedition's leaders were under pressure to return immediately to San Antonio since the Ranger company was scheduled to be mustered out of the U.S. Army after their service in the Mexican War.

Consequently, Colonel Hays and the other leaders discontinued the westward exploration, which already had taken much longer than expected, at Presidio del Norte. Besides that, an important observation had already made, that is, a wagon road to Chihuahua could not be built westward from San Antonio along the Rio Grande. The difficulties they had experienced between the Devil's River and Fort Leaton, especially the difficult terrain, were so great that Hays had been convinced that returning to San Antonio along the river was not a reasonable alternative. To this day, more than 150 years later, no road has been built along the American side of the Rio Grande and the lands along the river are still very difficult to traverse. Between Del Rio and Marathon, which are 175 miles apart on U.S. Highway 90, no paved road south of the highway has been constructed either to or along the Rio Grande. Simply put, Sam Maverick's Trail along the Rio Grande is still through a *terra incognita*.

> *Remaining 9 days in old adobe house 1 mi. E. of Leaton recruiting horses, buying mules, and provisions for the journey home. 8 cents per lb. for meal; $16 for powder; horse shoe nails $4 per lb. and 5 cents each.*

Having exhausted the men, supplies, horses and mules with which they had started west, the group rested close by Fort Leaton while preparing to search for the route for a wagon road to San Antonio. With a route directly east clearly impossible, the Expedition had little choice but to travel northeastward from Presidio del Norte toward home. How much information about their return route Hays and the scouts received from Ben Leaton and his associates or from the citizens of Presidio del Norte has never been documented, but Ben Leaton was confident enough of the Expedition's ability to return to San Antonio safely that his son returned with the expedition to attend school in the city. On October 31, 1848, more than two months after its departure from San Antonio, the men rode out of Presidio del Norte, Chihuahua, headed for home and a route over which a wagon road to Chihuahua and El Paso was possible.

> *Set off from Presidio del Norte for San Antonio.*
> *Oct 31 Going E.N.E.*

For some reason, the route out of the La Junta area has been disputed in many earlier books, including some which have included a return by way of Cibolo Creek. SAM's entry for the first day of travel should have left no doubt about the Trail's route. The only area which can be reached by riding 14 miles E.N.E. of Ojinaja (Presidio del Norte), Chihuahua is near or in the dry creekbed of Alamitos Creek, close to its junction with Cienagas Creek. Maverick did not describe this first return campsite as being on a creek, probably because Alamitos Creek was as dry there in 1848, except during floods, as it is today.

Swift[26] commented on the dispute: "This is important, for it does establish that Hays was the first Anglo-American, in scouting out the Alamitos Creek route, to use it as a link in the ultimately feasible road to the Gulf Coast."

> *Nov. 1, To creek at knob N 55 degrees, E 14 from Leaton's.*

North of the first camp, water can first be seen flowing down Alamitos Creek, so SAM's comment on a creek agrees with Alamitos Creek being part of the return trail. However, the November 1st campsite was in a broad creek bed with no structure which might be called a "knob." However, up San Jacinto Creek east of Alamitos stands San Jacinto Mountain, a quiescent volcano with a collapsed dome. A volcanic neck rises above the mountain on its west side, which fits SAM's description of a "knob." When located on topographic software from the National Geographic Society (NGS) 150 years later,[45] the volcanic neck of San Jacinto Mountain was found to be slightly east of 55 degrees of North from Fort Leaton, almost exactly the same location as SAM's "knob" at a creek. For those questioning the accuracy of Sam

Maverick's 1848 measurements and whether the Expedition traveled up Alamitos Creek from La Junta, his entry on November 1st strong supports a return route by way of Alamitos Creek. Equally as important, the agreement with the NGS program is powerful evidence of Sam Maverick's ability to accurately measure both the distance and the direction of the Expedition's route, confirming again the validity of his original entries. How SAM made the measurements was not reported in SAM's journal, so all we can do is assume that his surveying equipment could accurately calculate both mileage and directions traveled during the Expedition.

> *Nov. 2, Up same creek.*

From the San Jacinto Mountain area they continued up the broad valley of Alamitos Creek, still lined with the cottonwood, or "alamo," trees for which the creek was named, to this day and camped near present-day Perdiz. Upstream from this campsite, Alamitos Creek turns northwest because the eastern side of the valley is almost an unbroken solid bluff consisting of a thick layer of solidified lava, with the exception of a large canyon northeast of Perdiz. From this campsite, if Hays wanted to travel eastward, the group had to have ridden out through Robbers' Roost Canyon northeast of Perdiz, most likely over an old Indian trail up the canyon.

> *Nov. 3, Up creek 5 m. N.N.E. Then we strike over the hills, going by piles of stone, 15 m., and then about 5 m. over dog town plain - norther. Camp at N.E. extremity of plain south of mountain having on top two big stones and a zone.*
>
> *N.B. About 2 miles S.E. froom our camp and 3 or 4 from said mountain, on the east face of of another mountain is lead, etc. etc. to examine. The big knob with 2 stones etc. is about 5 ms. (back S.W.) from very sharp peak.*
>
> *Nov 4, In camp.*

The following day, November 3rd, would have been an arduous one since the Expedition traveled a long way from Alamitos Creek to their camp in the Paisano Mountains. Five miles above Perdiz, they left the creek's valley through the break in the long eastern wall called Robber's Roost

Canyon. At the head of the canyon lies a broad plain, now best known as the site of a phenomenon called the "Marfa Lights." After riding through the plain with "piles of stone," the Expedition crossed over a "dog town plain" and camped at what SAM called the "N.E. extremity of plain." At least three locations in the area qualify for the northeast extremity of the plain, but SAM's unusually specific description of the surrounding mountains defines the camp's location. The camp was located "south of mountain having on top two big stones and a zone," which was five miles southwest of a "very sharp peak." Anyone who has traveled the area between Fort Davis and Alpine, Texas knows that the "sharp peak" had to be Mitre Peak, a volcanic intrusion from which the surrounding softer rock has eroded to produce the appearance of a Bishop's mitre. Mitre Peak is strikingly different than the surrounding mountains and mesas in the area and probably served as a geographic marker for locating trails.

With SAM's description, the campsite had to be south of Twin Mountain and northwest of Black Peaks. The ride to the campsite across the plain was probably up Long Draw. Much to our regret, the route from Alamitos Creek to this camp could not be re-traced or the campsite photographed because the roads which follow Long Draw have been closed by the private landowner and no roads can even be seen north of the railroad tracks.

The camp's location in the Paisano Mountains was at a unique site compared to their subsequent campsites on Sam Maverick's Trail. The Paisano camp was the last camp located in a volcanic mountain or on the surface of a lava flow, which was a major change from the Expedition's travels during the previous weeks. Although their route through the Paisanos could be used by men on horses with pack mules, the route was too difficult for a wagon road for a good reason. The rugged and fragmented terrain where the Expedition camped had been the caldera of the Paisano Volcano.

Nov 5, N.E . In hills.

From the the Paisano Mountains, the Expedition rode northeast, down into the valley of Alpine Creek, now called Sunny Glen Canyon, where the creek flows north to join Muzquiz Creek. How close their route was to Muzquiz Creek is hard to determine since the largest hills in the valley are east of the creek above a broad plain. What is certain is that the Paisano volcano and the mountains of the Big Bend region were finally being left behind as they rode out of the canyon.

Nov. 6th, E.N.E.

Nov. 7th, 20 E. and 10 on trail (running E.N.E.). Camp in prairie in Norther.

As they rode first east-northeast, then east over the broad prairie of the Stockton Uplift between present-day Alpine and Fort Stockton, their trip was relatively easy except that no source of water was found. The Glass Mountains, bordering their route to the south, surround the Marathon Basin and were the last major hills or mountains that the Expedition passed by on their return to San Antonio.

Nov. 8th, Reach a spring in the Prairie, two days and four hours without water, going N.N.E. 6 miles.

Four hour after leaving their campsite, Maverick noted that the Expedition "Reach a spring in the Prairie" after two days of riding across the prairie where no source of water was found. Locating the "spring" proved to be one of the most important findings by the Expedition because what they had found was actually an oasis in the middle of the Stockton Plateau. With multiple sources of water, trees and a relatively protected camping site, the spring's massive production of clear, clean water had already been an important source of water for indigenous tribes, especially for the Comanches as they rode into Mexico on raids.

Locating Comanche Springs was a major discovery by the Hays Expedition since the springs quickly became an important stop for almost every wagon train on its way to either Chihuahua or El Paso. No other major source of water existed within miles of Comanche Springs, turning the springs into an oasis in the middle of a region where rain was a seasonal event. So within a matter of months, the springs were frequented by American Indian tribes, emigrant groups to California, traders with Chihuahua and U.S. Army trains.

Ultimately, to control travelers using the springs, the U.S. Army built Fort Stockton (its modern name) there and a city grew up around the fort.

Today, the city is the transportation hub of the TransPecos region with Interstate Highway 10 and several U.S. highway (U.S. 67, U.S. 285, U.S. 385) intersecting at Fort Stockton. Interstate 20 and U.S. Highway 90 are less than an hour away so that every region of far West Texas can be reached through Fort Stockton.

The story of what happened to Comanche Springs is a much sadder story. The major spring, the "Big Chief," is dry and enclosed on the deck of a swimming pool filled with city water. Comanche Creek. the outlet of the springs, is little more than a concrete-lined drainage ditch. A small county park below the pool has a few smaller, but dry, spring sites with a few trees. The springs water is now used for irrigation and the desert "oasis" no longer exists at Fort Stockton.

Nov. 9th, On trail (Durango trail) running here E. from point of mountains.

After riding only four miles east down from Comanche Creek from the springs, they camped again near a mesa on the Comanche trail.. After their difficult trip through the mountains of Big Bend region, what must have astonished the men was to find the broad Pecos River valley before them, an immense plain surrounded by mesas ten of miles apart. Even more striking was the lack of a physical feature identifying the route of the Pecos River since no trees or shrubs grow on the banks of the Pecos because frequent violent floods wash them away before growing tall enough to be seen.

The only physical feature visible far to the east was a depression between two mesas or mountains known as Castle Gap. Originally the destination of many trails created by prehistoric tribes who harvested salt from the lakes on the east side, the gap was by 1848 was best known as being part of the Comanche Road used by the Comanches on their way to plunder the northern settlements of Mexico. Over time, it would become part of the migrant trail to California (the "Upper Road"), a stagecoach stop on route to El Paso and even later on the Goodnight-Loving Trail through which thousands of cattle were driven to New Mexico. But in 1848 Castle Gap was primarily a landmark that was most useful because of its close proximity to Horsehead Crossing.

Nov. 10th, On trail N.N.E. to Pecos river. Find we are too high up.

This slightly confusing entry was difficult to understand initially, but a topographic map of the area provides the reason for the N.N.E. direction. Comanche Creek drains to the east from Comanche Springs until it approaches the Pecos River, where the creek turns sharply to the south to enter the river. To reach Horsehead Crossing on the "Durango trail," the Expedition was forced to turn to the northeast which explains the unusual change in direction. However, after arriving at the Crossing, the Expedition leaders decided that Horsehead was "too high up" for a river crossing and decided to ride south along the river in search of a better location.

The decision to search for a better crossing proved to be a mistake and was why SAM's entries were called "Seventy-four miles wasted down the Pecos." The five days and seventy-four miles of riding down the west side of the Pecos River, searching for a better place to cross the river, is the most likely reason why some writers in the past have reported that the Pioneer Expedition did not cross the Pecos at Horsehead Crossing, but at a crossing seventy miles downriver. Backtracking the daily mileages from Live Oak Creek upriver to where Maverick's report "crossed with a stretched rope" supports Horsehead Crossing as the place where 1848 expedition finally crossed over to the east side of the Pecos. His journal entries for the next few days (November 11th to 15th) describe where they traveled and what they found before returning to Horsehead Crossing to cross over to the east side of the river.

"Seventy-four miles lost down the Pecos"

Nov. 11th, Down Pecos S.E. No trail. Old grass in rock.

Nov 12th, Down river S.E. and to 2nd trail and four (miles) on it. Overhaul fifteen San Migl. (Santa Fe) traders who say there are no more trails crossing the Pecos above the one 20 miles up.

The November 12th entry by SAM was his last until November 17th after the Expedition had crossed the Pecos at Horsehead Crossing and camped several miles down the east side of the river. To make the November 12th entry more comprehensible, SAM's entries are divided into three parts for discussion of what he reported or was trying to report.

The first comments were about meeting the Santa Fe traders, who provided both information and food for the Expedition. After riding south along the west side of the river, searching for a ford which would be suitable for a wagon road crossing on the the Pecos River, they met fifteen traders from Santa Fe on the third day, probably near Escondido Springs or Creek (near Bakersfield, Texas). The traders told Hays that no hard-bottom crossing of the Pecos existed below Horsehead Crossing, forcing the Expedition members to ride back up the west side to Horsehead. Their search down the west side of the Pecos seeking a crossing had been a mistake, so the many miles of travel looking for a ford had been "wasted." That explains why Maverick referred to the effort as "Seventy-four miles wasted down the Pecos."

However, learning that Horsehead Crossing was the only good Pecos River crossing along this stretch of the river ultimately led to Horsehead becoming a critical part of the wagon road between San Antonio and El Paso. The leaders of the Pioneer Expedition may have considered those five days and seventy-four miles down the west side of the Pecos a waste, but the information about Horsehead Crossing proved to be invaluable for the many travelers who would soon be crossing the Pecos at Horsehead. Besides the information about the only hard bottom crossing of the Pecos River (Horsehead) and the food the traders sold them, the Expedition's contact with the San Miguel traders had an unexpected benefit, i.e. Hays and Maverick learned from the traders that a road along the west side of Pecos River existed between Santa Miguel, New Mexico to the area around Escondido Creek that flowed into the Pecos. . The road probably had been used by indigenous tribes for decades, if not centuries, along the Pecos River as a trading route to the ancient pueblo near Terrero, New Mexico.

In retrospect, what the Expedition leaders learned from the traders during their brief meeting makes it hard to defend Maverick's comment about "miles wasted down the Pecos". Besides learning that Horsehead Crossing was the only good Pecos River crossing in the area, especially near Castle Gap, they were also told about two sources of salt located east of the Crossing. In addition, the presence of Santa Fe traders south of Horsehead showed that a road adequate for carrying supplies and goods from Indian raiders was present from the Crossing upstream to Santa Fe, almost five hundred miles north of the traders' campsite. The traders also described some of the lands along the Pecos River between Horsehead Crossing and Santa Fe. That information would have been useful in negotiating the Compromise of 1850. establishing the border between the States of Texas and New Mexico.[46]

Nov 12th (continued)

N.B. 12 or 15 miles above the upper or big Durango trail on E. side of Pecos and 1 league from it is Salt Lake where there is an abundance of salt dry; and some 50 miles above same trail on W. side is a salt creek from some spring distant from river an in hills. These men came down the Pecos to trade in bread with the Indians etc. The Pecos water is quite salt but I like to drink it. Bread made up with it rose in a manner which led me to suppose that there was soda in it.

In the *noto bene* (N.B) or "note well" addition to his November 12th entry (second part), SAM included information unrelated to the Trail's route which he had obtained from the Santa Miguel traders, the Expedition's scouts or by personal observation. This part of the note apparently was intended to summarize the sources of salt on both sides of the Pecos River near Horsehead Crossing. The information about the salt creek west of the river above the trail was probably provided by the traders since SAM mentions that the men had come down the Pecos from that direction. The description of a salt lake on the east side "above the upper or big Durango trail" matches the location of present-day Juan Madrona Lake. No mention is made of a salt lake on the east side below the Crossing where the smaller Soda Lake is found, suggesting that the traders had not traveled down the east side.

The salty taste of Pecos River water and how much he liked its taste is one of the few personal comments SAM included in his journal. His observation that the water might contain soda because "bread made up with it rose" indicates that the salt was more than plain sodium chloride. The interest in salt makes little sense in the 21st Century, but in the mid-1800s several battles were fought over ownership of salt sources, including one in which Sam Maverick was involved. His detailed description of the places where salt could be found is no surprise for those times.

Many earlier reports have given credit to different explorers, besides the Comanches of which the crossing was part of their road to Mexico, for locating Horsehead Crossing while traveling eastward but without giving specific mileages for where they reached Horsehead Crossing. The information obtained from the San Miguel traders by Maverick provides specific distances for the Hays expedition's travels in search of a hard-bottomed crossing. When measured on a modern topographic map, there is little doubt about the Hays group having been the first to cross the Pecos River at Horsehead Crossing and confirm its location. Confirming their finding is the fact that no other hard-bottomed crossing has been found down the Pecos River as far as Live Oak Creek. The Whiting-Smith reconnaissance in 1849 (after crossing on a log bridge near Pecos Springs) with Dick Howard as its scout rode west along the Pecos River up to Horsehead Crossing, after which they rode up the Comanche road to Comanche Springs. Because of the problems at Horsehead, future crossings of the Pecos River were built by ferry, pontoon bridge and finally modern bridges so that Horsehead's days as the major hard-bottomed crossing of the Pecos were short-lived.

Horsehead Crossing to Granger Draw

> *Crossed with a stretched rope. Stream 40 ft. wide and 20 ft. deep. Soil very superior. Stunted, prickly bushes and wood very scarce. Irrigation could be practice here extensively. Grazing good but not equal I think to Medina etc.*

This writer's first visits to Horsehead Crossing made the Expedition's crossing of the Pecos River very difficult to imagine when the river was "40 ft. wide and 20 ft. deep," and required a stretched rope to reach the east side. Driving from a paved highway down the dusty dirt road to the Crossing, two or three irrigation canals without water were found but no crops were being grown and even though the soil still appeared to be superior. At the crossing, many stunted, prickly bushes still surrounded the area and wood except for fence posts was scarce to absent. Grazing obviously was no longer "good" since no foraging or grazing animals of any kind were seen. And the amount of water flowing down the Pecos River was not enough for a creek. The lack of water was due to the dams having been built upstream from Horsehead, primarily in New Mexico, and several years of drought in the Pecos River valley.

Our two photographic trips to the Crossing a few years later dramatically changed the writer's opinion of what the Expedition must had faced in 1848. Our first photographic trip back was during a period when the Pecos River basin had just had its largest rainfall in almost fifty years. The effects of the rain were to turn the drive down the dirt road to the Crossing into an adventure. After passing over the second irrigation canal, our car started to sink slowly into the muddy road. With discretion being the better of valor, we stopped only long enough for Jim to photograph Castle Gap and for me to turn the car around without ending up in a ditch.

Even the drive back over the muddy road to a paved highway was a challenge, but it also taught us a lesson about the effects of rain on the soil around Horsehead Crossing. The mud that was caked over and under the car was like glue and took weeks before being removed. Besides the mud problem, we also saw what crossing the Pecos in 1848 must have been like downstream on a bridge over the river near an 1848 campsite. Swollen with floodwaters and flowing over its banks, the Pecos River was 50 to 60 feet wide and over 20 feet deep. Since no trees were present near the bridge to anchor ropes, much the same as at Horsehead, it was hard to imagine how the Expedition's members had managed to get men, horses and mules across a river "40 feet wide and 20 feet deep."

On the second trip to Horsehead, the road to Horsehead was muddy, but not enough to prevent our reaching the Crossing to take photographs. But how the river's appearance had changed since the writer's earlier visits! Massive floodwaters had risen at least five feet above the river banks, sweeping away much of the existing vegetation and removing almost all the human garbage that had accumulated for years. A metal gate and fence on the east side had disappeared and only a few bushes still grew on the side of the banks, stripped of their leaves. The floodwaters and the sand it carried had re-landscaped Horsehead Crossing into a site completely different from our earlier visits. If we had had any question as to why the crossing had a long history of being difficult to cross for generations, our second trip provided the answer.

Although no date was given in SAM's journal for the day they crossed the Pecos River, November 16th, 1848 is the most likely day since the first dated entry after November 12th was for November 17th after they crossing Horsehead. In addition, the most likely location for their next camp was near Soda Lake below the Crossing despite SAM's not mentioning the salt lake. SAM's description of the land on the east side of the Pecos fits what is much the same today, except for good grazing, and the campsite approximates the location obtained by backtracking SAM's mileage from Live Oak Creek.

Nov. 17th, Down the Pecos.

Continuing their ride down the valley the following day, they camped below small cliffs on the Pecos River where the mesas begin to enclose the river valley for the first time. The broad floodplain of the Pecos River, which began upstream in New Mexico gradually narrows downstream as the Pecos approaches its lower canyons and their meandering course to the Rio Grande.

Nov. 18th, By lime stone bluffs.

Although the distance between the limestone bluffs and the river varies here, from this day until the Expedition left the Pecos River valley at Live Oak Creek, the trail was between the bluffs of the mesas surrounding the river. This day's ride was across a fairly open plain on the east side until they camped near present-day Iraan, Texas, where the eastern mesa bluffs reach down almost to the Pecos River at what became Pontoon Crossing.

Nov. 19th, S.E. Tight squeeze to get along at foot of mountains. Camp at Live Oak grove.

Nov. 20th, Lay by at the grove.

On the trail between the campsites for November 18th and 19th, three cliffs on the east side of the Pecos River can be seen from the west. The formations of the plateaus above the cliffs are easily seen, including where the rock has broken off and fallen down the cliff to form a talus. The writer was quickly convinced of the existence of a "tight squeeze" below one of the cliffs when he almost drove off the cliff into the Pecos while looking at the huge boulders in the talus above the road. The River Road on the east side is much closer to the river than one realizes, but its proximity only becomes obvious when the bushes beside the Road are seen to be growing horizontally, not vertically, from the cliff. After the near miss into the Pecos, a few minutes was required for his heartbeat to return to normal, after which the drive down the River Road to Live Oak Creek was relatively easy on what must have been a good trail.

The live oak grove where the Expedition camped in 1848 is gone and the groves of oak trees are rare, except at a few places up Live Oak Creek. No trees of any kind were found at the Expedition's campsite. All that remains there now are eroded limestone rock and a variety of desert plants growing on the surrounding land.

Nov. 21st, Down Pecos 2 miles; then up cr. N.E. 5.

The second day spent at the grove was most likely used by the scouts to search for a route eastward by which they could return to San Antonio. A search down the Pecos River this day would not have found a suitable route home because, except for a few miles below Live Oak Creek, even trails were blocked by high bluffs with a trail or route to the east. The only route that could be used to ride eastward would have to start from Live Oak Creek, the only reliable source of water flowing into the Pecos River. So they rode up Live Oak Creek and camped at its junction with a canyon now called Mailbox Draw.

The importance of Live Oak Creek as a source of water for men and animals cannot be underestimated. The next expedition westward to explore the border, the Whiting-Smith Reconnaissance, owed its survival to finding water at the creek after two days of searching for a spring or waterhole on the Edwards Plateau as the Hays Expedition had found. A route to the north was not possible because the creek ends at bluffs above the creek. Only a ride up Mailbox Draw to the northeast might lead them home. The Expedition was the first of thousands that stopped at Live Oak Creek on its way westward and was one of the reasons that Fort Lancaster was built a few miles away.

Nov. 22nd, E.N.E. (Good way) 15.

The Expedition's ability to ride a "good way" this day is no surprise since the terrain up Mailbox Draw to the plateau rises both gradually and is relatively unobstructed until the draw turns abruptly to the north west of Howard Draw. Today its northward turn passes under Interstate Highway 10 and reflects the historical importance of Mailbox Draw.

Initially the draw was the route by which the Johnston-Van Horne expedition built the wagon road from San Antonio to El Paso. Later, roads into or above Mailbox Draw were an integral part of the road to El Paso. Later, a road was built down the bluff on the south side and ultimately was given the name, U.S. Highway 290, a name it maintains today as a bypass route to the ruins of Fort Lancaster. Despite construction of Interstate Highway 10 on the north side of the draw, a county road still passes down the draw to Live Oak Creek and ultimately to the Pecos River.

With their discovery of Mailbox Draw as a route to the northeast and Howard Draw, the 1848 Hays expedition found part of the wagon road from San Antonio to El Paso that still exists over 150 years later. Although its significance as part of a wagon road was lost when the railroad was completed in 1883, Mailbox Draw is still part of the road west to Chihuahua, El Paso and California as either Interstate Highway 10 or U.S. Highway 290 which run parallel to Mailbox Draw.

Nov. 23d, E.N.E., E. and E.S.E. At mustang camp and here lose Hays fine horse and 5 others.

Once on the divide above the draw, the trip down to camp in Howard's Draw should have been relatively easy. although no mention of a water source was made. From Howard Draw, the trail was essentially due east and close to, if not through, present-day Ozona, Texas to a campsite on the plateau east of Ozona. Locating the mustang camp mentioned by SAM has not been possible, but the plateau east of Ozona has multiple waterholes, any of which were adequate for a mustang camp. Although SAM did not say whether Hays "fine horse" had been lost or broken down, other reports of the Expedition have indicated that Hays' horse had been stolen by Indians.

Hays must have noted the existence of many waterholes on the plateau since he later recommended a route from San Antonio up the San Saba River and across the plateau to the Whiting-Smith Expedition when it departed in February 1849. Whiting and his group quickly learned a hard lesson about waterholes on plateaus, as many travelers in the region have since 1849: waterholes are not a reliable source of water. During a photographic trip west on IH-10, the writer and photographer were lucky to find a waterhole full of water to photograph. Why were we lucky? That was the only time that the writer had seen water in the plateau's waterholes during the previous nine years of driving past the waterholes. The only reliable source of water on the plateau has been from water wells, not from surface water, between Live Oak Creek and the North Llano River.

Nov. 24th, E.S.E. and S.E. water hole - Breaking down and losing 6 or 7 more animals.

Although the route to this waterhole on the 24th could have been down any of several draws, the Expedition's most likely route was by way of Willow Draw to its junction with Granger Draw, which is called the Devil's River on Texas highway maps. The relationship of the draw to the Devil's River was first noted by SAM who called this campsite the "supposed head of the Devil's River." Water from Granger draw does drain down to meet the upper Dry Devil's River, so the location is as good as any to call the Devil's River's "supposed head."

This night was special for the members of Expedition because it was the last time when all members of the Expedition camped as a single group. The following day, the San Antonio members with Hays and Maverick headed home on a southeasterly route. Highsmith's group of Rangers and Delaware guides rode northeast up a draw for their return to the Castell Ranger camp. After reaching either the South Concho River or San Saba River, they returned to Castell to re-join the other Rangers in Highsmith's company, but only after suffering a great deal of hardship compared to the San Antonio party's return.

Expedition Separates for Return

Since Highsmith's group of Texas Rangers and Delaware Indians returned directly to their camp at Castell without Sam Maverick, SAM's journal entries could not have include any information about the Rangers' return. The best source of information about Highsmith's contingent was recorded by John Henry Brown in his 1880 book.[36] Despite some minor inaccuracies, such as where they separated from the Hays party and how many members returned with each group, the difficulties that Highsmith's company faced on its route back to Castell were clearly described by Brown. Based on SAM's record of the return home of the other fourteen members, including Hays and Maverick, the San Antonio members had a much easier and safer trip home than Highsmith's group to Castell. Both routes would soon be part of roads to the west, but a route close to that used by the Hays/Maverick group was included in an important section of the "Lower Road," the year-round road from the Texas Gulf Coast through San Antonio to El Paso.

Highsmith's Rangers to Castell

"They struck the Pecos at at the Horsehead crossing, and followed that stream down to Live Oak creek, where Fort Lancaster was afterwards established. It was in that locality that the command separated. Twenty-eight of the San Antonio party started in a direct route for that city and safely arrived at their destination. Colonel Hays, with six men, returned by way of the Las Moras and also got in safely, but both parties suffered much.

From Live Oak creek Captain Highsmith bore across the country towards the source of the South Concho. On the way, on one occasion, some of the men fell in the rear on account of their failing horses, and at night camped in thicket of small bushes. While asleep at night a party of Indians rode over them, seizing a saddle and some other articles and successfully stampeding their horses. On foot they overhauled the company at camp next morning. On the head of the South Concho they encamped for the night. One of the sentinels fell asleep and at daylight it was found that the Indians had quietly taken off thirteen of their horses. Thenceforward about half the men traveled on foot.

At the head of Brady's Creek, these men, clad only in their now tattered and torn summer garments, encountered a violent snowstorm. Captain Highsmith, with a few men, pushed forward to his quarters on the Llano, to relieve the anxiety of the country as to their safety, correctly conjecturing that intense anxiety among the people must exist on account of their prolonged absence. The other men remained shivering in an open camp for five days. The sufferings of both parties were terrible. Their beef was exhausted and wild game was their only food, but it was abundant in deer, antelope and turkey. On the forty-seventh day from Fort Leaton the last party reached the camp on the Llano. Thus with forty-seven days each on the outward and inward trip and 18 days at the fort, they had been absent 112 instead of 60 days. The re-united company was marched to

Austin, and on the 26th day of December, discharged, their terms of service having expired."

Author's Comment:

Unfortunately, the events which occurred during the Castell's contigent return by a separate route back to Castell are based on what the survivors told friends and family about that experience, except for Brown's comment that the Rangers at Castell were finally discharged from the Texas Mounted Volunteers on December 26, 1848. However, despite their status as former members of the U.S. Army, the contributions of Captain Highsmith's Company to the expedition should be credited to their frontier experience as Texas Rangers since that was the critical factor in surviving the exploration of the *terra incognita*.

The description of Highsmith's return to Castell by Brown is the major source of information about the Castell contingent of the Pioneer Expedition's return home. Although some of the individual members from Castell were well known as Indian fighters and frontiersman, little has been written about when and how they returned to be mustered out of the Mounted Volunteers. At least three members of Highsmith's group soon joined the Whiting-Smith expedition and upon its completion were the first Americans to have explored all of the Texas-Mexico border from the Devils River up the Rio Grande to El Paso.

Hays/Maverick to Las Moras Springs

> *Nov 25th, We with Col. Hays, 14 of us, part from Capt. Highsmith's Company at water holes, supposed head of Devils' river and some 20 miles south of Concho, and go S.E.*

Granger Draw is near the top of the Devil's River watershed on the Edwards Plateau. From there, the small hills with broad valleys are progressively more deeply cut as one goes southward. Except for a line of hills found in that direction, "going S.E." from Granger Draw should have been relatively easy compared to the country they had traveled for months, but the San Antonio group's first camp in the Dry Devil's River valley near where Hudspeth Draw meets the river. As we learned, describing a route through this part of Texas is complicated by the existence of not one, but two, Dry Devil's Rivers, both of which flow into the main Devil's River. To prevent confusion, the two rivers will be identified as either the upper or the lower Dry Devil's River. The November 25th campsite refers to the upper Dry Devil's River where waterholes full of water were found on our trip there despite its name.

Nov. 26th, Sunday. 8 m. SSE and 4 SSW down dry creek and to hole. Kill a hog.

SAM's entry about their travel from the upper Dry Devil's River valley is confusing again because he refers to going "down" a dry creek. What SAM meant by "up" and "down" repeatedly created difficulties in locating the trail during our re-exploration, but this day he most likely meant over the ridge south of the Dry Devil's and down a branch of East Buckley Draw to camp at a waterhole. The big change this day was the group's return to where food, in this instance a hog, could be supplied by hunting wildlife. The hog meat must have been part of a change in their diet since SAM had not mentioned hunting for food since leaving Presidio del Norte. Finding feral hogs in 1848 is worth noting since their population has exploded in Texas to become a major source of damage to crops.

Nov. 27th, SE over Live Oak and Lime stone hills and pretty valleys. 3 deer killed.

To reach this camp, the San Antonio group crossed over or around the gentle hills along the lower Dry Devil's River valley to camp in or near Buffalo Draw based on the distance and direction of travel. SAM's comment about the pretty hills and valleys is appropriate for Buffalo Draw where the abundance of grass still attracts deer. In 1848 the venison from three deer may have been an even bigger reward than the hogmeat. Compared to their diet of tunas and bear grass soup on the Rio Grande section of the Trail, eating hogmeat and venison must have felt like a return to Paradise.

Nov. 28th, SSE. Pretty and rich live oak valleys. Small mesquite grass. No water.

At Buffalo Draw's east end, several other draws, which were probably the "pretty and rich live oak valleys" described by SAM, drain into the Buffalo where it turns to the northeast. Wittenberg Draw, which enters from the southeast, rises gradually to the divide between the Devil's River watershed and the West Nueces River watershed. Typical of their campsites on other divides in the Edwards Plateau region, no springs or other source of water were found on this divide where the top of Wittenberg Draw of the lower Dry Devil's River valley meets the top of Crooked Draw of the West Nueces River valley.

> *Nov. 29th, Norther morning. Found water at 2 miles and met in trail two Comanches with Philip _____ a captive, and 14 stolen animals. Camp at pond head of W branch of Nueces.*

Their trail down to the West Nueces River probably was an existing Indian trail because, after finding water at a spring, they rode down the trail to meet two Comanche Indians with a young boy they had captured and fourteen stolen animals. One of the Comanches escaped during a fight, but the other one was captured along with the boy and the animals. After the fight, they continued down the trail to camp at a pond near the origin of the West Nueces where the other Comanche escaped. The night of the 29th was interrupted when Indians were seen near the camp. An attempt by one of the guards named Perfecto to shoot them produced unexpected results.

> *Nov. 30th, South with our captive and Philip and the horses. Last night, one of our guard, Perfecto _____ shot at Indians prowling 200 yards from our camp, killing a mule - shot thro' the saddle.*

This morning they awoke to find that Perfecto's shot had been accurate, but what he had seen moving the night before and thought was an "Indian," actually was one of their mules, which he had shot through its saddle. Perfecto's killing the mule must have been a humorous event after the Expedition's many grueling weeks of exploration,

The San Antonio group continued their travels down the West Nueces River, into which small, wooded valleys feed at regular intervals, usually with little if any waterflow into the river. No mention is made of a "dry camp" so they must have camped on the river.

> *Dec'r 1st, SSE big trail and over rocky and overflowing beds of branches*

> of the Nueces and thro' several very pretty valleys. Camp at the coral mote and spring - League of fine mesquite and live oak land here. Prime land, timber and water and very suitable for a ranch, & fat deer.

SAM's description of a "SSE big trail" over rocky and creek beds with an abundance of water flow suggests that the group had ridden down the West Nueces to the Kickapoo Springs area below which a stable source of water flow is found. The camp at a spring surrounded by "prime land very suitable for a ranch" could fit several locations in area today and was probably their last camp in the West Nueces River Canyon. Below the river's canyon the land spreads out into a prairie and only Las Moras Mountain to the south of the Canyon separated the Hays/Maverick group from Las Moras Springs.

> Dec. 2. 1848 This day about S. 10 degrees E. 15 miles to Las Moras Spring and 8 to dry creek, no water.

December 2nd, 1848 was in effect the day that the Chihuahua-El Paso Pioneer Expedition ended. The Highsmith contingent had separated from the Hays/Maverick party several days ago on its way back to Castell. The San Antonio group, which had started the original expedition in August, 1848, rode down to Las Moras Springs, then east to camp at a dry creek on the trail between Las Moras Springs and San Antonio. From this site, they would no longer be exploring new lands since the lands along their route were had been traveled for centuries by Indians, Spaniards and early day Texans.

Today, to the east of this location, the lands have been changed more by human settlement since 1848 than any other section of Sam Maverick's Trail. Although the region west of San Antonio is primarily used for agricultural activities, significant tourist, hunting and industrial activities have been and are being developed on both sides of the old route. Today U.S. Highway 90 passes through lands which are so different from those in 1848 that Sam Maverick would have a difficult time finding the way back to his home on the San Antonio River, assuming he could get through the many fences which crisscross the region. However, the major factor which limited the development of the country west of San Antonio has not changed since Hays and Maverick returned home over 160 years ago, that is, the availability of an adequate water supply where prolonged drouths occur periodically.

Leona River Back to San Antonio

After camping east of Las Moras Creek, Hays, Maverick and the San Antonio members of the Pioneer Expedition returned to the Expedition's starting place, two and a half months after their departure from Las Moras Springs and a month and a half later than originally planned. Of the San Antonio men who left the city on August 27, 1848 on their trip to Castell, the only missing member was Doctor Wahm, who had "gone crazy" and ridden off into the wilds of the Big Bend. The return to San Antonio would be relatively easy since the trail from the Nueces River was well known to Sam Maverick, who had surveyed extensively in the surrounding region. Although the section of their route from the Nueces River to San Antonio had been traveled for centuries while under Spanish control, only Castroville and three small Alsatian villages had been established west of San Antonio under the Republic of Texas. Maverick's brief comments about this section provide very little information about what had been the western frontier of Texas republic and the site of many conflicts between American Indian tribes, Spaniards and early Texas settlers besides more recent battles between Mexico and Texas.

> *Dec. 3rd Came to water in 2 m. and breakfast. Pass water again in afternoon. Camp at hole in creek running S.E. in prime elm and mesquite lands. Camp 1 m.*

> *Dec 4th To west bank of Nueces.*

Their return east from the Las Moras Springs area was across rolling hills covered with grass and trees, but most of which has since been replaced by mesquite trees and cacti. From the north, springs and rivers flow down from the Edwards Plateau through several canyons, including the Nueces Canyon through which the Pioneer Expedition had traveled from Castell, providing multiple sources of water for the men and their animals. To the south, the Anacacho Mountains rose up from the prairie a few miles southwest of Uvalde, Texas not far from the site of Fort Inge on the Leona

River. Those mountains separated the old road to the presidio on the Rio Grande (and later Fort Duncan at Eagle Pass) from the upper road to Las Moras Springs. The road to the springs, where Fort Clark would be built, became part of the original San Antonio to El Paso road that the Johnston-Van Horne expedition built.

> Dec. 5th Leona within a mile of head.
>
> Dec. 6 Lay by in sleet and norther.

What Sam Maverick called the "Leona" is the Leona River whose waters flow through today's Uvalde, Texas and provided water for Fort Inge, built below a rocky peak beside the river. The fort's site had been used by nomadic Indian tribes for centuries for camping as well as for signaling from Mount Inge. The location was near the old smuggling road between San Antonio and San Juan Bautista on the Rio Grande that had been a presidio since the early days of Spanish Texas. Originally the road had been called General Woll's Road after the Mexican general who marched his army over the road to San Antonio where he captured Sam Maverick and several other citizens defending the city.[10] Those Texas captives walked back down the same road to Mexico City, ultimately reaching Perote Prison where they were imprisoned. During the Mexican-American War, an American general, General John Wool, chose the same route for marching his troops to Presidio del Rio Grande (Guerrero, Coahuila) and into Mexico.[47] That is why the road has been referred to as both Woll's Road and Wool's Road, confusing historians and laymen alike.

Fort Inge, first built and garrisoned below the hill on the Leona River in the spring of 1849, was used intermittently by both the U.S Army and Texas Rangers for the protection of the nearby settlers and travelers on the San Antonio-El Paso Road. Periodically, campaigns against both marauding Indians and Mexican bandits were also based there. However, the fort was never a stable military post as noted in 1854 by Robert E. Lee, who passed through the fort with a party which included four camels:[17] "...as was usually the case with frontier forts, there were no structures for defense, except a stockade of mesquite logs about the stables, which were open thatched huts. The post consisted of a dozen buildings of various sizes... all scattered about the border of a parade ground, pleasantly shaded by hackberries and elms. The buildings were rough and temporary, some of the officers' lodgings being jacal. But all were white-washed and neatly kept, by taste and discipline." Considering Lee's description, it is no surprise that Fort Inge was soon abandoned since both Fort Clark at Las Moras Springs and Fort Duncan at Eagle Pass on the Rio Grande were larger, better-built installations located at or near more heavily traveled Indian trails used for raids into Mexico.

With multiple sources of water and fertile soil on a trade route to Mexico, the lands near the fort was among the first to be settled west of Castroville. However, the native tribes, who had hunted and lived in the river canyons north of the fort for centuries, frequently used trails through the canyons to attack the new settlers. Those attacks on the American settlers continued for over thirty years after the 1848 Pioneer Expedition passed by the Leona River, ending only when all of the tribes had moved north of the Hill Country.

From the Leona River, the San Antonio group rode eastward to the Rio Frio where the original road to El Paso turned to pass north of the Anacacho Mountains on its way to Las Moras Springs. The Woll/Wool Road, located a few miles south of Fort Inge, passed south of the Anacachos on the opposite side of the mountains from the road to Las Moras. A more direct route to Eagle Pass, Fort Duncan and Piedras Negras, Coahuila soon replaced the original Spanish road to Presidio del Rio Grande.

Dec 7th to Sabinal Creek.

Sabinal Creek (or River) is one of many creeks and rivers which originate from springs on the southern edge of the Edwards Plateau. The valleys of the Nueces, Frio, Sabinal and Medina Rivers are among the most scenic and fertile found along Sam Maverick's Trail, which is why several towns and communities on the rivers were the first to be established west of San Antonio. Despite the new railroad's construction creating a few new towns, Highway 90 west from San Antonio still closely follows the original road through most of the towns built on those creeks and rivers.

Dec 8th to Seco Cr. (Warfield's Post).

Warfield's Post was an early frontier trading post north of D'Hanis on Woll's/Wool's road between San Antonio and Mexico. Although not as well established as the original Alsatian town of Castroville in 1848, D'Hanis was another early Texas settlement associated with Castroville as were its neighbors in Vandenberg and Quihi. In 1849, shortly after the Pioneer Expedition's visit, Fort Lincoln was built on the bluff above Seco Creek across from the trading post. Fort Lincoln, a new frontier fort built to protect the nearby settlers, was the connecting point between the line of forts from Fort Worth on the Trinity River south to an east-west line ending at Fort Duncan on the Rio Grande.[48]

From Warfield's Post, the Hays/Maverick group rode east, crossing Hondo Creek, before passing through the small settlements at Vandenberg and Quihi. Although Vandenberg on Verde Creek was abandoned during a prolonged drought and moved south to a new townsite, Quihi has survived as one of the original Alsatian settlements. The settlers of all four towns, D'Hanis, Vandenberg, Quihi and Castroville, persevered despite repeated attacks by the Comanches and other tribes until the region was finally pacified in the early 1880s. The continued existence of the original communities into the 21st Century is powerful evidence of the courage and tenacity of those first Alsatian who founded the first villages west of San Antonio.

Dec 9th, Castroville.

Built and settled by Alsatian immigrants on the riverbank above the Medina River, this small community, where they had many friends, must have been a welcome sight to the San Antonio explorers. Besides their return to civilization, the group's arrival in Castroville also meant that home was less than twenty-five miles away. After surviving a much longer and more dangerous exploration than originally expected, riding down the streets of Castroville must have been especially rewarding to the men from San Antonio who had been gone from their homes for several months. A few hours ride down a well-established road would bring them home.

Dec 10th, San Antonio.

The original Expedition, projected to require two months for the round-trip to both El Paso and Presidio del Norte, had taken three-and-a-half months just to reach Presidio del Norte, ended this day with their arrival in San Antonio. Only Doctor Wahm, who had "gone crazy" and run off in the Big Bend, failed to return with the original members in December 1848. However, good fortune found Doctor Wahm when he was captured in the *despoblado* by a friendly Indian tribe with whom he lived for a year. In return for providing medical care to its members, the tribe brought Doctor Wahm safely back to San Antonio a month before his wife was to marry another man, after assuming he had died. When the privations the Expedition's members had suffered, and the incredibly difficult terrain they had crossed, are considered, the safe return of the original San Antonio expedition members was at least a minor miracle.

6

SECOND EXPLORATION OF TEXAS-MEXICO BORDER

Reconnaissance to El Paso del Norte **by Whiting/Smith**

After the Texas Mounted Volunteers (Rangers) were mustered out of their frontier camps at the end of 1848, the U.S. Army built a line of forts from the Trinity River south to D'Hanis. Despite no official explanation, one can assume that protection of the Texas frontier must have been transferred to the U.S. Government as of January 1, 1849 and the Texas Rangers were no longer responsible for its defense. In addition, two forts built during the war with Mexico, Fort Inge (Uvalde) and Fort Duncan (Eagle Pass), were re-garrisoned with infantry troops as part of the U.S. Army's new responsibility.

The Commander of the U.S. troops in Texas, General William Worth, had his headquarters at the Alamo which the Army had repaired and expanded. With the failure of the 1848 Hays Expedition to find the route for a wagon road along the Rio Grande, one of the major problems confronting General Worth was the lack of an east-west road to El Paso where the Third Brigade was to build its headquarters. Consequently, he ordered two young Topographical Engineers, Lieutenant William H.C. Whiting and Lieutenant W.F. Smith, to undertake "A Reconnaissance from San Antonio de Bexar to El Paso del Norte," the second exploration of the Texas-Mexico border, which Whiting described in his very detailed diary during the expedition.[41] Their specific objective was limited to locating a route suitable for a wagon road along the Rio Grande from La Junta de los Rios (Presidio del Norte) to El Paso del Norte in Mexico. Since the 1848 Pioneer Expedition had already confirmed that a road could not be built along the river between the Devils River and Fort Leaton, Whiting and Smith were limited to exploring the final section of the border between Texas and Mexico.

San Saba River to Davis Mountains

Based on the advice of Colonel Jack Hays, Whiting and Smith chose to start their westward reconnaissance by way of the San Saba River on which Spain had built the abandoned Presidio San Saba. However, they soon learned that the large number of "waterholes" on the Edwards Plateau which Hays had found while returning to San Antonio were no longer present beyond the headwaters of the San Saba River. The absence of waterholes, springs and flowing creeks on the plateau forced the expedition to ride across the plateau from the San Saba without water for men and their stock. They finally found water after riding down Mailbox Draw to the flowing waters of Live Oak Creek. The seasonal presence of waterholes, and all too often the total absence of surface water on the plateau, persists to this day.

After traveling down Live Oak Creek to the Pecos River, Whiting and Smith crossed over to the west side of the river and rode up to Horsehead Crossing. From the crossing, they used the Comanche road to reach Comanche Springs to camp before deciding to take a different route west than the Hays group had. That decision was probably due to the absence of water on the plains after leaving Muzquiz Creek for "two days and four hours" before reaching Comanche Springs as Maverick had noted in his journal. The new route directly west toward the Davis Mountains was a marked improvement over the 1848 expedition's trail since water was found within a few miles at Leon Holes, possibly at Barillas Springs, and in a flowing stream from San Solomon Springs. But the route west to that stream led to a unexpected confrontation with an Apache raiding party returning from Mexico.

After multiple threats from the Apaches, five Apache chiefs led Whiting, Smith and Howard, followed by their men and animals from the springs up a trail into the Davis Mountains so the Apaches could parley with the Americans. After camping on Limpia Creek near the "Painted Trees," Whiting described the meeting with the Apache chiefs and confirmed that the U.S. government's obligations under Article XI were a major reason for the 1849 reconnaissance:

"They asked if they would be disturbed in the possession of their lands. I told them no, provided they were peaceable. They were curious as to our relations with Mexico. I satisfied them as far as I could, but prudently refrained from touching on all points, for the slightest allusion to that part of our treaty which relates to the restraining of Indian depredations and the restoration of stolen captives and property would have been the signal to fight. I was in no condition to enforce what I said; and when it is considered that we were but thirteen armed men, and five of these provided with but a single shot, our scanty stock of provisions reduced to short allowance, badly armed and mounted, and important public information dependent upon our return, this concealment on my part will be pardoned."

That night after making camp, the U.S. expedition managed to ride off from their campsite at the Painted Trees , without arousing the tribe's attention, even though it was not far from the Apaches' camp. Thus the Whiting-Smith group survived the night by hiding in a pile of rocks several miles from Limpia Creek even though the Apaches attacked their vacated campsite later that night. From its campsite in the rocks, the expedition rode south down what Whiting thought was Cibolo Creek, but must have been the north branch of Alamitos Creek. They were able to ride down Alamitos Creek with little difficulty, except for the lack of food, to reach Fort Leaton safely without an attack by the Apaches. The last days of their ride down Alamitos Creek , according to Whiting, followed the trail that the Hays expedition had used on its return to San Antonio , confirming that they were in Alamitos Creek, not Cibolo Creek.

Fort Leaton to El Paso del Norte

The Whiting-Smith reconnaissance was well received by Ben Leaton and his men at the fort despite their own limited supplies. After visiting Presidio del Norte (today's Ojinaja, Chihuahua) that had continued to exist only because the Apaches had already stolen everything of value from its people. With Leaton's help, the expedition was able to replace enough of its animals and supplies to complete exploration of the section of the border up to El Paso that the Hays expedition had failed to explore. The distance from Presidio del Norte to the El Paso area was relatively short and their only concern was whether it was suitable for building a wagon road along the river.

With the addition of two of Leaton's men for assistance, the Whiting-Smith expedition followed the route Cabeza de Vaca had traveled up the Rio Grande from La Junta de los Rios to the floodplain of the Rio Grande below El Paso del Norte. What they found reflected both the regions' geology and how completely the Apaches controlled that section of the border. The river above La Junta was in a mountainous region that is basically two mountain ranges through which the Rio Grande has eroded a channel. The lands up to the first range, called the Eagle Mountains on the U.S. side, included two *fortalezzas* (presidios) built on the Mexican side that had been abandoned and were falling apart due to neglect. In addition, on the American side of the river, two large winter villages of the Apaches were found that had been recently vacated.

The second mountain range, the Quitman Mountains, were also cut through by the river and more difficult to cross than the Eagle Mountains. However, once crossed, they found themselves on the floodplain below El Paso del Norte where another Apache winter village, also recently vacated, had been built. From the Apache village, they continued their travels up to the "island," or isleta, created by a change in the channel of the Rio Grande. The result of the river's shift southward was that the Presidio San Elizario, one of the Spanish presidios in Spain's "northern line of defense," was now in the United States. Whiting commented that the first words he heard from the residents was, "We are Americans."

In effect, the American exploration of the its border with Mexico was complete with its expedition's arrival at San Elizario. That small town and its adjacent missions (Socorro and Ysleta) had already been occupied by Doniphan's Missouri Volunteers during the war. However, the former presidio at San Elizario would be re-built by U.S. troops and serve as the first county seat of El Paso County since no city existed on the U.S. side across from El Paso del Norte.

Arrival of the expedition led by Whiting and Smith at San Elizario finished the first American exploration of the Rio Grande border between the Devils River and New Mexico territory. It is worth noting that at least three members of the 1849 reconnaissance expedition, Richard A. Howard, John Hunter and William A. Howard, were the first Americans to have explored the entire length of the Texas-Mexico border between Del Rio, Texas and El Paso, Texas. However, the official Boundary Survey of the Rio Grande/Rio Bravo between Mexico and the United States would not be completed until several years later. However, it is also important to emphasize that the Whiting and Smith reconnaissance had not found a route adequate for construction of a wagon from San Antonio to El Paso, just as the Pioneer Expedition of 1848 had failed to find a suitable route.

New Route Back From El Paso del Norte

The story of the first American exploration of the Texas-Mexico border ended with the arrival of the Whiting-Smith expedition at San Elizario, formerly Presidio San Elizario under Spanish rule but now part of the United States. The course of the Rio Grande had been moved southward by flooding, switching an "island" of originally Spanish towns to the north side. Except for finding the route for a wagon road along the Rio Grande, the explorations had been successful in many ways. That objective is still impossible since the complex and rugged topography on the U.S. side of the river between Del Rio and El Paso, Texas makes road building too expensive even it was possible.

However, the expeditions were successful in several ways, not the least of which was surviving their expeditions. Besides locating the border, the region was found to have been depopulated by decades of Indian depredations in Mexico. Too many trails leading from the United States into Mexico had been found to make recording their locations worthwhile. The 1848 Hays expedition found only one inhabited site below Presidio del Norte. Only Rancho (formerly Presidio) San Carlos had managed to survive, primarily by acting as a trading post for the Mescaleros. At La Junta del los Rio, Presidio del Norte (Ojinaja) had permanent inhabitants while in the United States, only Fort Leaton across from Presidio del Norte had occupants, primarily due to the efforts of Ben Leaton.

Consequently, a new effort to build a wagon road to San Antonio would have to start upon Whiting-Smith's return home. Fortunately, its return trip was through lands with obstacles they knew to avoid, allowing them to search for a new route to San Antonio. The information they supplied was enough to convince General Kearney that the "southern" route was where Johnston and Van Horne expedition should construct the wagon road to El Paso. The stories of Whiting-Smith's return to San Antonio and the even more extensive reports of Johnston-Van Horne's efforts while building the road to El Paso deserve more than a brief summary here. The final stories remain to be told in the future as part of the U.S. Army's achievements in settling the West and preventing Indian depredations in Mexico.

7

THE BORDER AFTER SIGNING OF TREATY

Before Jack Hays could lead the expedition in its exploration of the new border, several events had to occur, especially since the U.S. negotiator, Nicholas P. Trist, had been fired by President Polk before the Treaty had been signed. Upon receipt of the treaty negotiated by Trist, President Polk and his Cabinet discussed the best course for finalizing a peace treaty. Based on the intense opposition to the war by many Americans, Polk chose to send the treaty to the U.S. Senate for ratification.

Ratification by the U.S. Senate and President

Despite the President's support, the initial response by the Senate to expose the opposition by several members to ratifying the treaty. Because of the opposition, Senator Sam Houston of Texas moved that the debate be held in secret, the reason why no record exist as to what occurred during the Senate's discussion of ratification. However, after several changes had been made by the Senate under pressure from President Polk, the U.S. Senate ratified the Treaty of Guadalupe Hidalgo with amendments on March 10th by more than the two-thirds margin required and sent it back to the President. Six days later, President Polk ratified the treaty with the amendments and sent the U.S. version of the treaty to Mexico for ratification by its Congress.

Ratification by the Mexican Congress

Much has been written about the hostility between the two governments because of the war and the U.S victory to cover the subject even superficially. However, Brantz Mayer[6, p. 429] provides an accurate picture of the relationship between the countries after the peace treaty was sent to Mexico for ratification by the Mexican Congress.

"On the 25th May, a brilliant *cortege* of American cavalry was seen winding along the hills toward Queretaro as the escort of American commissioners, who were welcomed to the seat of the government by national authorities, and entertained sumptuously in an edifice set apart for their accommodation. The town was wild with rejoicing. Those who had been so recently regarded as bitter foes, were hailed with all of the ardor of ancient, and uninterrupted friendship. No one would have imagined that war had ever been waged between the soldiers of the north and south who now shared the same barracks and pledged each other in their social cups. If the drama was prepared for the occasion by the government, it was certainly well played, and unquestionably diverted the minds of the turbulent and dangerous clashes of the capital at a moment when good feeling was most needed.

Congress was in session when our commissioners arrived, and on the same day the Senate ratified the treaty, which, after a stormy debate, had previously been sanctioned by the Chamber of Deputies. On the 30th of May the ratifications were finally exchanged, and the first installment of indemnity being paid in the city of Mexico, our troops evacuated the country in the most orderly manner during the following summer."

Mayer also answered the question as to how the new government used the three million dollars in indemnity paid by the U.S.A.[6, p. 430] But the three millions, received opportunely for indemnity, were no doubt used judiciously by the authorities, while the men of property and opulent merchants leagued zealously with municipal authorities to preserve order until national reorganization might begin." The steps taken to reorganize a new government included election of a new Constitutional President and Chief Justice of the Supreme Court, reinstallation of the capital in the city of Mexico, putting down a rebellion by General Paredes in Guanajvato, and stopping rebellious outbreaks regions outside the capital city.

What is clear from Mayer's description is that the new government had a friendly relationship with the United States which provided indemnity funding activities critical to maintaining peace in Mexico under very unstable conditions. Many tasks remained to be done after ratification of the treaty, not the least of which was formation of a binational Boundary Commission to survey the final border between the two countries. That effort required several years , especially since neither country had a major presence in the lands along the border controlled primarily by the Apaches and Comanches. Defining the boundary was also complicated by the use of an inaccurate map (Disturnel's) as part of the Treaty of Guadalupe Hidalgo. However, the most important task facing both countries was the need to terminate attacks in Mexico by "hostile tribes" based in the United States. Completion of that goal would require decades of both independent and joint campaigns by the American and Mexican armies.

Completion of the Hays Expedition's Goals

Finding Route for San Antonio-El Paso Wagon Road

The return of the Whiting-Smith reconnaissance from El Paso del Norte had a new responsibility, that is, serve as scouts seeking a feasible route for a wagon road between the two cities. Considering the difficulties both of the early expeditions had faced, Whiting and Smith were reinforced and re-supplied for their new mission. Due to a combination of luck, the frontier skills of their Texas cohorts and the extensive knowledge of Richard Howard obtained during three trips over the wild, uninhabited lands of far West Texas, a route suitable for the road was found a few days before an expedition under Colonel Johnston and Major Van Horne was to have departed San Antonio to build the new road, possibly by a northern route.

With new information about the best route to El Paso, that is, a route with water sources adequate for large wagon trains, General Kearney decided that the "lower route" discovered by Whiting-Smith should be the route by which a wagon road was to be built from San Antonio to El Paso. Within days, the first U.S. Army troops, animals and wagons left San Antonio on its way to rendezvous at the "head" of the Leona River (Uvalde), a few miles north of Fort Inge, with the last group of Van Horne's Infantry.

Once the entire expedition had finally been assembled with the Topographical Engineers under the command of Colonel Joel Johnston and the Infantry under the command of Major Jeffrey Van Horne, the Engineers under the leadership of Colonel Johnston and Lieutenant William Smith, left to survey the best route for a road to El Paso.[49]

Transfer of Border Protection to U.S. Army

Due in part to its obligations under Article XI of the peace treaty, responsibility for defending the Texas frontier was transferred from the Texas Rangers (Mounted Volunteers) to the United States Army on January 1, 1849. However, with the return of American troops from Mexico, the U.S.

Army built forts along the western frontier of Texas as its responsibility for the frontier's defense required. A report by Lieutenant William Whiting[49] described the status of the new frontier forts and what would be required for the U.S. Army's defense of the western frontier of Texas.

Frontier Forts Along the Road to El Paso

Migration to the western frontier by both native-born and new immigrants gradually pushed the large Comanche tribe, whose main source of food and support had been the massive buffalo herds of the central plains, away from the early Texas settlements.[20] The indigenous Apache tribes had already been forced off the high plains by the Comanches into the desert and mountains of the Southwest. So, in order to survive, the Apaches increasingly depended upon raiding northern, and even central, Mexico.

Thus, the inclusion of Article XI in the Treaty of Guadalupe Hidalgo, by which the U.S. Government assumed control of the "savage tribes" in the new territories, including returning their captives and stolen property to Mexican owners, was found to be a particularly deceptive concession of the Treaty.[16] The Americans, who supposedly "won" the war with Mexico and "usurped" the northern territories originally claimed by Spain prior to Mexican independence, was burdened with the responsibility for controlling the "savage tribes" in their new territory. Although the few Hispanic people living in those lands had some knowledge as to how many indigenous tribal members lived near the new Texas-Mexico border, the United States government clearly did not comprehend that the total population of border tribes was approximately 160,000, far more than the number of Americans living west of central Texas.

No group was more affected by its new responsibilities to control the savage tribes than the U.S Army. In his book on old forts of the Southwest, Hart[17] described the situation in what he called "The Early Days":

"When the Mexican border was pushed southward to the Rio Grande, the American Army found itself caught in the middle. On one hand there were the Indians and the lawless. On the other, the settlers and politicians who wanted protection from the Indians and the lawless."

The greatest achievement by the U.S. Army under such difficult circumstances was to build the first east-west road across America's newly acquired lands between San Antonio and El Paso. The new road was more than a route along which forts could be built to protect travelers and prevent Indian depredations in Mexico. The road was also a much shorter land route between the Gulf of Mexico and the Pacific Ocean, creating a new bicoastal region in the United States. With the discovery of gold in California, the new San Antonio-El Paso road led to explosive economic growth in the Southwest. Completion of the road was an achievement far greater than the attention it has received.

Ultimately, creation of a stable border without continuous conflicts would depend upon cooperation between the governments of the United States and Mexico. Major problems, including organizing a new government in Mexico, had to be solved. The peace treaty ratified by U.S Congress, then the Congress of Mexico, had to become "the law of the land" in both countries. The most difficult problem was the Republic of Mexico's lack of funds to meet the many obligations created by the war. And the 1848 Hays expedition along the new border could not leave San Antonio until at least the final border had been agreed upon. Defining and securing the border between Mexico and the United States has been a problem without resolution that has persisted into the 21st Century.

Epilogue

The Chihuahua-El Paso Pioneer Expedition was created by a group of San Antonio businessmen to find a route for a wagon road to Chihuahua before another city in Texas could build one. The financial benefits of trade with Chihuahua was why they raised the initial funds for the expedition and hired Jack Hays, the famous Texas Ranger and hero of the Mexican war, to lead the expedition. However, the project was complicated by the U.S. government's obligations to Mexico under Article XI of the Treaty of Guadalupe Hidalgo, specifically preventing depredations in Mexico by hostile tribes based in the United States. So, what had started out as a purely financial venture quickly turned into an expedition with three goals. First, locate the new border between Texas and Mexico. Second, find a route along that border (the Rio Grande) over which a wagon road could be built to Chihuahua and El Paso. Third, find the trails that hostile tribes from the United States used to enter Mexico.

In terms of its 1848 objectives, the Hays expedition was both successful and unsuccesful. No route for a wagon road along the Rio Grande from the Devil's River up to Presidio del Norte was found, a result that was also confirmed for a route up the river from Presidio del Norte to El Paso del Norte by the Whiting-Smith expedition that followed. Except for short sections, no road along the Rio Grande on the American side has been built by the 21st Century.

On its return home, they were more successful by locating sites, especially reliable sources of water for men and their stock, that were important to subsequent expansion westward. Those sites included the Alamitos Creek valley, where the main Chihuahua Road was built, Comanche Springs, Horsehead Crossing, and Live Oak Creek, all of which would have major roles in the growth of western Texas. Unfortunately, they were also able to find many trails leading down into Mexico that were used by American tribes to raid the ranches, towns and people of Mexico. That information would prove to be valuable to the U.S. Army in developing forts and camps to prevent attacks in Mexico but also on the settlers who moved into the American Southwest.

The expedition's contributions were critical to building a road to El Paso, which would create a road from the Gulf of Mexico to the Pacific Ocean, that proved to have major economic impact as the Gold Rush to California produced a major migration to the West. The Chihuahua Road also led to very active trade between Chihuahua and San Antonio, just as the original organizers had planned. But from a broader viewpoint, the Hays expedition managed to survive an exploration through previously unexplored lands controlled by several Indian tribes and return home safely, a significant achievement by itself.

The final results of the 1848 Chihuahua-El Paso Pioneer Expedition can be summarized by repeating Jack Hays response when asked what the expedition had found: "Lots of mountains. Lots of deserts. No water."

Methods Used to Locate Sam Maverick's Trail

Human expertise

Surveyor members of the Expedition:

As described in Measuring America,[50] geodetic surveys of new lands were possible "using triangulation to calculate distance, celestial observation to establish locaton, and barometric pressure to indicate height" by 1848. Richard (Dick) Howard had attended West Point (Class of 1845), where Ferdinand Hassler, the first superintendent of the Coast Survey, had taught after emigrating to America from Switzerland. The surveying techniques Hassler had taught at the US Military Academy were almost certainly known to the Expedition's leaders either through Howard or general usage by surveyors. In addition, Gunter's chain had been used to survey new western lands since 1785 and Sam Maverick's personal chain is in a Texas state museum. Thus, by the time the Pioneer Expedition left San Antonio in 1848, the techniques required to determine the distances they had traveled on the Trail were well established.

Despite his well-known expertise as a surveyor, in the past questions have been raised by historians about the accuracy of the mileages recorded in Maverick's journal. The accuracy of SAM's mileages can be demonstrated by the total mileage, 482 miles, that he recorded for the return home to San Antonio from Presidio del Norte. If the same distance were measured today based on mileage using modern highways built near or along Sam Maverick's Trail, the total is surprisingly close, i.e. 462 miles. However, the Expedition trip north from Fort Stockton to Horsehead Crossing and down the eastern side of the Pecos River added thirty miles to the total for the return compared to a modern route along U.S. Interstate Highway 10 directly east from Fort Stockton to the Pecos River. When those thirty miles are subtracted from SAM's total, the 1848 distance is 452 miles, only ten miles less than today's route on modern highways! The accuracy of SAM's mileage is almost unbelievable when 1848 surveying techniques are compared to modern satellite mapping.

Consequently, the directions and mileages recorded in SAM's journal were assumed to be accurate enough to locate the Expedition's route over 150 years later. In contrast to Expedition's efforts, we used modern gasoline-powered vehicles, instead of horses and mules. However, even with modern vehicles and accurate maps, re-exploring the Trail proved to be more physically demanding than expected and topographic maps failed to show many of the obstacles along the Trail, especially in and along rivers and draws. Re-exploration of Sam Maverick's Trail, where the Expedition had traveled in 1848, required a ground-level search to accurately locate the exploration's route and the difficult terrain through which the Expedition had traveled.

Regional experts and local residents:

Even using modern topographic and satellite maps, the search for Sam Maverick's Trail had been underway only briefly when the need for advice and support from individuals, who had "been there and done that," was obvious. The most valuable support and enthusiasm unquestionably came from Louis Aulbach, supreme canoeist and author of several books, the most important of which is about the canyons of the Lower Rio Grande Canyon.[37] Beyond a question, the westward route of the Trail along the Rio Grande could not have been found without Louis' willingness to respond to tens, if not hundreds, of e-mails. The section from the Devil's River to Big Bend National Park was by far the most difficult section to locate as well as to access on the ground. Louis' extensive experience, both floating down the rivers and hiking through the country west of the Devil's River, provided critical information about where the Expedition might have traveled. He also generously provided his and Dana Enos expertise by leading the exploration of Sanderson Canyon, about which he has written in the River Canyon Country section.

Re-exploration of the Devils River section of Sam Maverick's Trail was a special problem since that part of the river is now covered by the waters of Lake Amistad in the Amistad National Recreational Area (NRA). We were fortunate to find Joe Labadie, an archeologist and the Cultural Resources Program Manager at Amistad NRA, who is an expert both on the Devil's River and the wagon roads through the Lake Amistad area. Joe not only provided us with information and photographs from his files, but also personally took us by boat up the Devils River arm of Lake Amistad for photographs.

Labadie's monograph about the Amistad NRA was particularly useful in differentiating between a "trail" and a "wagon road."[51] Trails could be traveled by men on horses using pack mules to carry supplies for their support, just as the Pioneer Expedition had done in 1848, but the load that mules carried was limited compared to wagons. For wagon travel across western Texas to be established, a necessity if forts were to be built and supplied, a road larger and more level than a horse trail had to be built. Even on the roads, multiple horses or mules were required to pull wagons large enough to transport supplies for the forts as well as cross-country commercial traffic. That is why many trails, but few roads, are found on the region's mid-19th Century maps.

Serendipity played an unexpected role in re-exploring the Trail's section along the Rio Grande River. Due to the writer's unexpected illness, a photographic trip was cut short, giving us time to stop at the Terrell County Courthouse and meet Judge Dudley Harrison, owner of the large ranch in which Sanderson Canyon is located. Although he had retired, "Judge Dud" was at the courthouse and agreed to help us search his 35,000 acre ranch for possible pictographs in the Canyon. Dudley's support for the hike from the Rio Grande up Sanderson Canyon in search of Indian art was critical to our discovery of pictographs in the canyon. In addition, Dudley's driving the writer around his ranch and along The Rio Grande Wild and Scenic River provided insight as to where the 1848 Expedition had been forced to ride along the Rio Grande.

If not for the Fosters, Billie and Billy, the Indian pictographs in Sanderson Canyon might not have been found. Billie, a State Park Guide at Seminole Canyon State Historical Park, told the writer that her husband, Billy, who grew up in the area west of Langtry, had heard about Indian paintings on the walls of Sanderson Canyon. Billy Foster not only obtained permission for us to access the photographic site but also drove us to the junction of Lozier Canyon with the Rio Grande, a critical location for an accurate re-exploration of the Trail. If we held any doubts about topographic maps' failure to show all of the physical obstacles existing at ground level, our trip with Billy Foster into Lozier Canyon removed those doubts.

Topographic techniques

Distance measuring device for maps:

When first seen in a National Geographic Society catalog, a device called the Map Mouse by Lingo® appeared to be a gimmick, but after learning how to use the device on a map of Texas, the Map Mouse was the first accurate method used to compare mileages on modern maps with those recorded by SAM during the 1848 Pioneer Expedition. By setting the map's scale on the Mouse, distances between possible campsites were measured on the maps of the Expedition's travels. The accuracy of the mileages that Sam Maverick recorded in 1848 first became apparent when the Map Mouse was used for scouting trips to find the original trail. Much to the writer's surprise, when the mileage of the first section of Sam Maverick's Trail from San Antonio to Castell, then down to Las Moras Springs was measured on a modern map with the Map Mouse, the total distance measured by the new technique was only one mile greater than the mileage Sam Maverick had recorded in 1848! Despite the device's accuracy for initially locating the 1848 campsites, the Mouse was not accurate enough to locate the original campsites, so the re-exploration of the Trail on the ground required the use of computer-generated topographic maps.

Computer software and GPS locations for 1848 campsites:

If a "breakthrough" occurred while searching for the route of Sam Maverick's Trail, it was finding a computer software program called Topo USA® developed by deLorme, a mapping software company located in Falmouth, Maine. With the release of Version 4 of the Topo USA® program, for the first time it was possible to compare 2-dimensional (2D) with 3-dimensional (3D) views of a map simultaneously on the same computer screen.[52] By approximating the Expedition's trail on the 2D view based on SAM's journal entries, a "virtual trip" through the lands was possible on the 3D view. In many cases, what had been a logical route on the 2D view was clearly impossible when seen in the 3D view. For example, the Expedition's leaders would not have chosen a route up and over a large hill or mountain when the expedition could have ridden up a draw or across a relatively flat plain.

In addition, the location of a campsite with its elevation was shown on the 2D map and could be compared to the same location on the 3D map, which was critical information for retracing and photographing the 1848 campsites on Sam Maverick's Trail. Most of the expedition's campsites were found on the computer's map based on its GPS locations and initially "seen" on the 3D map before a trip was made to the campsite for photographs. Although occasionally misleading, recognizing the location of a campsite on the ground, which had not been seen before except on the 3D map view, frequently surprised us, especially since the source of the campsite locations on the original trail had been recorded over 150 years ago.

As the terrain through which the Expedition had traveled in 1848 became rougher and more isolated, 3D map views were no longer adequate for locating the original trail, especially in several places where SAM's journal was either very brief or difficult to interpret. In addition, the deLorme maps did not show many of the present-day names for locations shown on the 3D views. To increase the likelihood of finding an original campsite before photographic trips, another computer program, the Texas version of Topo!® from the National Geographic Society (NGS), was used to find the names of locations in the area of the 1848 campsites.[45] Besides having more detailed and up-to-date labeling, the NGS program also provided more specific topographic detail. Since a 7.5' USGS map was included in the NGS program, GPS locations were more easily determined and printed out on a map before re-exploring the trail. Several variations of the routes which the Expedition might have traveled could be printed out and easily measured, increasing the accuracy of our efforts to find Sam Maverick's Trail. However, despite the modern software mapping programs, either from deLorme or from the National Geographic Society, which increased the precision of our search for the trail, we quickly found on the many roads, trails or creek bottoms that no topographic map could replace searching for the trail in person. What had been obvious and clear on a map too often turned out to be totally incorrect at ground level. Photographic sites which could be clearly seen on a computer map led to more than one humbling experience which required hiking around or over limestone hills or driving aimlessly through countryside without a distinguishing feature.

During the re-exploration while photographs of the campsites on the Trail were being taken, Global Positioning System (GPS) locations were documented at the photographic site using a Garmin GeckoR GPS locator and recorded in a daily journal. The approximate GPS locations for the original 1848 campsites are based on the daily record in Maverick's 1848 journal after being found using computer topographic software. The campsite locations were then recorded on a map of Texas to show the route that the original 1848 Pioneer Expedition followed during its exploration.

Problems in locating the Expedition's route:

The Pioneer Expedition's original route as recorded in SAM's journal was basically a surveyor's journal with a brief list of miles and the direction that the Expedition had traveled, making location of individual campsites difficult to define precisely. SAM's earlier journals had been more descriptive, but, according to his family and friends, his grief over the loss of his daughter, who had died shortly before his joining the Expedition, had severely affected him. The brevity of his journal has been explained by that grief, but his extensive experience as a surveyor in early Texas produced an accurate record of the mileage covered, even if his description of the spectacular 1,300 mile trail was surprisingly limited.

The major problems with finding the route were caused by Maverick's failure to record either the daily mileage or direction to several campsites. Too often, only a description of what the Expedition had done that day was noted. Although the daily entries were adequate for most of the Expedition's trail, the route was most difficult to accurately locate where SAM failed to record critical details about the campsite's location. Those campsites or trail segments whose exact location were difficult to determine from his journal, especially those which have been questioned in previous publications, had to be approximated by the use of such techniques as "backtracking" from a previously confirmed campsite. So, depending upon the amount of information available, the locations of the 1848 campsites range from "best guesstimates" to very specific locations.

Photographic documentation:

Why was photographic documentation of the re-exploration necessary? The main reason was to confirm that the writer and photographer had personally re-explored Sam Maverick's Trail. In addition, words alone cannot adequately describe what photographs of the terrain can more accurately portray. Finally, the photographs, as spectacular as most are, provide only a limited perspective of the vast and spectacular lands explored by the 1848 Pioneer Expedition.

After the 1848 campsites had been located, photographs were taken to document the campsites on the original Trail. Although three of the campsites were not photographed due to our inability to access the sites, their GPS locations confirmed the accuracy of SAM's 1848 journal entries as well as our re-exploration the original Pioneer Expedition campsites. Jim Keller's photographs are not only spectacular by themselves, but also support our findings about the route of Sam Maverick's Trail.

These photographs are not included with this text. The main reason is that the color images are too large and too numerous to fit into the text. Many of the images are panoramas that, even if they fit, would not accurately portray the spectacular scenery where the photographs were taken. In addition, the photographs were taken over a twelve year period during which major advances in both digital photography and digital printing occurred, thereby creating incompatibilities that prevented their inclusion in the book without major changes in the photographs.

Another book containing the color images from the re-exploration is under the direction of Jim Keller Photography.

Re-Exploring Sam Maverick's Trail

The original plan to re-explore Sam Maverick's Trail had been to create a modern travelogue of the 1848 Expedition's trail with photographs by Jim Keller, but, just as I had learned during my research career, starting a project is very frequently like opening Pandora's Box. What at first was planned as a simple re-tracing of an event occurring over a century and a half ago turned into an multi-year investigation of a very complex period in Texas and American history. Although somewhat familiar with the Chihuahua roads and the Treaty of Guadalupe Hidalgo, I was ignorant of the economic impact that opening a road from Chihuahua to San Antonio had as well as the difficulties associated with the exploration and defense of western Texas. In addition, I learned that the first two explorations in 1848 and 1849 were by two groups of veteran Texas frontiersmen. Even if I had known about the contributions of Texas frontiersmen to the first expeditions, nothing could have prepared us for the complex terrain of the lands along the Rio Grande and around the Big Bend. As Lieutenant Whiting wrote in 1849.[85] "The whole of the neighboring region of the Big Bend requires thorough reconnaissance. The geology, geography, and topography of it are unknown."

During our re-exploration, we learned more about the geology, geography and topography of the Big Bend region than was imaginable, much of which has been described in the preceding pages. But, even after traveling thousands of miles in and through the region, we are convinced that most of Whiting's "neighboring region," the fascinating lands along the Big Bend's border, should be studied by more expert and knowledgeable professionals in the fields of geology, geography, anthropology and archeology in the future.

Article XI of the Treaty of Guadalupe Hidalgo

(Quoted from Griswold del Castillo, Appendix 2, p. 190.[16])

"Considering that a great part of the territories which, by the present treaty, are to be comprehended for the future within the limits of the United States, is now occupied by savage tribes, who will hereafter be under the exclusive control of the Government of the United States, and whose incursions within the territory of Mexico would be prejudicial in the extreme; it is solemnly agreed that all such incursions shall be forcibly restrained by the Government of the United States, whensover this may be necessary; and that that when they cannot be prevented, they shall be punished by the said Government, and satisfaction for the same shall be exacted; all in the same way, and with equal diligence and energy, as if same incursions were mediated or committed within it's (sp) own territory against it's (sp) own citizens.

"It shall not be lawful, under any pretext whatever, for any inhabitant of the United States, to purchase or acquire any Mexican or any foreigner residing in Mexico, who may have been captured by Indians inhabiting the territory of either of the two Republics; nor to purchase or acquire horses, mules, cattle or property of any kind, stolen within Mexican territory by such Indians;

"And, in the event of any person or persons, captured within Mexican territory by Indians, being carried into the territory of the United States, the Government of the latter engages and binds itself, in the most solemn manner, so soon as it shall know of such captives being within it's (sp) territory, and shall be able so to do, through the faithful exercise of it's (sp) influence and power, to rescue them, and return them to their country, or to deliver them to the agent or representative of the Mexican Government. The Mexican Authorities will, as far as practicable, give to the Government of the United States notice of such captures; and it's (sp) agent shall pay the expenses incurred in the maintenance and transmission of the rescued captives; who, in the meantime, shall be treated with the utmost hospitality by the American Authorities at the place where they may be. But if the Government of the United States, before receiving such notice from Mexico, should obtain intelligence through any other channel, of the existence of Mexican captives within it's (sp) territory, it will proceed forthwith to effect their release and delivery to the Mexican agent, as above stipulated.

"For the purpose of giving to these stipulations the fullest possible efficacy, thereby affording the security and redress demanded by their true spirit and intent, the Government of the United States will now and hereafter pass, without unnecessary delay, and always vigilantly enforce, such laws as the nature of subject may require. And finally, the sacredness of this obligation shall never be lost sight of by the said Government, when providing for the removal of the Indians from any portion of the said territories, or for it's (sp) being settled by citizens of the United States, but on the contrary, special care shall be taken not to place it's (sp) Indian occupants under the necessity of seeking new homes, by committing those invasions which the United States have solemnly obliged themselves to restrain."

Approximate GPS Locations of 1848 Campsites

Rendezvous at Las Moras Springs
San Antonio to Las Moras Springs (August 27–September 18, 1848)

1. August 27 / Head of Olmos Creek:	N 29° 33.37'	W 98° 33.99'
2. August 28 / Cibolo Creek:	N 29° 47.03'	W 98° 43.04'
3. August 29 / Sisty's Creek:	N 29° 57.43'	W 98° 43.04'
4. August 30 / Fredericksburg:	N 30° 14.99'	W 98° 50.85'
5. August 31 / Baron's Creek:	N 30° 42.15'	W 98° 56.12'
6. September 1-3 / Highsmith's Camp:	N 30° 42.29'	W 98° 57.52'
7. September 4-5 / Up Llano River:	N 30° 39.68'	W 99° 06.57'
8. September 6 / Comanche Creek:	N 30° 39.37'	W 99° 08.95'
9. September 7 / Above James River:	N 30° 38.59'	W 99° 18.94'
10. September 8 / Llano River Junction:	N 30° 29.50'	W 99° 45.24'
11. September 9 / South Llano River:	N 30° 23.67'	W 99° 53.16'
12. September 10 / Camp above springs:	N 30° 10.83'	W 99° 51.09'
13. September 11 / Road to Nueces River:	N 30° 04.57'	W 99° 55.71'
14. September 12 / Main Nueces River:	N 29° 55.96'	W 100° 00.10'
15. September 13 / Down Nueces River:	N 29° 52.92'	W 100° 01.08'
16. September 14, 15 / Old Stone Mission:	N 29° 32.22'	W 100° 00.78'
17. September 16 / Waterhole:	N 29° 19.69'	W 99° 56.85'
18. September 17, 18 / Las Moras Creek:	N 29° 18.50'	W 100° 25.04'

Total miles to Las Moras (SAM): 285

Westward to La Junta De Los Rios
Las Moras Springs to Fort Leaton (September 19–October 22, 1848)

19. September 19 / San Pedro Creek:	N 29° 23.41'	W 100° 40.29'
20. September 20 / Turkey Creek:	N 29° 21.41'	W 100° 53.56'
21. September 21 / Mouth, Devil's River:	N 29° 28.15'	W 101° 3.18'
22. September 22 / NW side, Devil's River:	N 29° 34.40'	W 100° 58.66'
23. September 23 / Ravine Devil's:	N 29° 39.46'	W 100° 55.45'

24. September 24 / Up Devil's River:		N 29° 39.12'		W 100° 59.07'
25. September 25 / Pecos River divide:		N 29° 51.75'		W 101° 13.67'
26. September 26 / To the Pecos:		N 29° 51.96'		W 101° 24.05'
27. September 27-28 / Lower Pecos River:		N 29° 53.47'		W 101° 30.19'
28. September 29 / Cross Pecos:		N 29° 52.96'		W 101° 31.34'
29. September 30 / New trail:		N 29° 47.72'		W 101° 37.41'
30. October 1 / To water in rocks:		N 29° 54.21'		W 101° 48.33'
31. October 2 / Banks of Rio Grande:		N 29° 48.08'		W 101° 51.27'
32. October 3 / Out Rocky Creek:		N 29° 48.06'		W 101° 51.85'
33. October 4 / Up river to spring:		N 29° 48.96'		W 101° 58.58'
34. October 5 / Lookout Peak:		N 29° 48.63'		W 102° 5.70'
35. October 6 / Down creek to holes:		N 29° 51.43'		W 102° 12.28'
36. October 7 / To impassable ravine:		N 30° 1.54'		W 102° 19.35'
37. October 8 / Worst hills; Apache trail:		N 29° 57.85'		W 102° 12.41'
38. October 9 / Travel up canyon:		N 29° 50.83'		W 102° 11.01'
39. October 10 / Canyon Mezcal Creek:		N 29° 52.76'		W 102° 19.20'
40. October 11 / 1.5 miles to big trail:		N 29° 51.61'		W 102° 32.52'
41. October 12 / Down creek to plain:		N 29° 44.33'		W 102° 52.85'
42. October 13 / Travel down plain:		N 29° 29.11'		W 103° 7.24'
43. October 14 / To camp with water:		N 29° 10.93'		W 102° 59.53'
44. October 15 / Creek to Rio Grande:		N 29° 10.59'		W 102° 59.80'

In Mexico Around Big Bend / October 16–19, 1848 (No GPS locations available)

45. October 16 / Down big Comanche road (camp at spring in Mexico)   18 SSW
46. October 17 / Quit Comanche road (camp on branch):   20 (W, WNW, NW)
47. October 18-19 / Up irrigable creek (Rancho San Carlos):   10 (6 NW, 4 W)

In camp (on hill opposite San Carlos)

48. October 20 / Camp in road at creek:		N 29° 17.79'		W 103° 57.71'
49. October 21 / Camp at hole:		N 29° 23.74'		W 104° 10.14'
50. October 22 / Re-cross (Fort Leaton):		N 29° 32.62'		W 104° 19.68'

Return East to Home

Presidio del Norte to San Antonio (October 30–December 10, 1848)

51. October 30 / In Presidio del Norte:	N 29° 33.64'	W 104° 22.33'
52. October 31 / LV Presidio del Norte:	N 29° 39.52'	W 104° 11.67°
53. November 1 / Alamitos Creek:	N 29° 49.19'	W 104° 2.06'
54. November 2 / Up same creek:	N 29° 55.12'	W 104° 0.79'
55. November 3-4 / Up creek, over hills:	N 30° 29.00'	W 103° 44.41'
56. November 5 / N.E. in hills:	N 30° 30.67'	W 103° 33.69'
57. November 6 / In hills:	N 30° 38.40'	W 103° 15.57'
58. November 7 / To camp in prairie:	N 30° 47.81'	W 102° 53.59'
59. November 8 / Spring in prairie:	N 30° 53.64'	W 102° 52.75'
60. November 9 / Durango Trail:	N 30° 57.05'	W 102° 49.25'
61. November 10 / Horsehead Crossing:	N 31° 14.15'	W 102° 29.44'

"Miles lost down the Pecos" (No GPS locations included)

62. November 11 / Down west side of Pecos
63. November 12 / Down river S.E. Pecos to trail
64. November 13 / Overhaul 5 Sante Fe traders
65. November 14-15 / Back to Horsehead Crossing

66. November 16 / Crossed Pecos River:	N 31° 9.70'	W 102° 24.20'
67. November 17 / East side Pecos River:	N 31° 0.20'	W 102° 7.78'
68. November 18 / By limestone cliffs:	N 30° 54.27'	W 101° 52.76'
69. November 19-20 / "Tight squeeze":	N 30° 39.49'	W 101° 44.23'
70. November 21 / Down Pecos, up creek:	N 30° 43.88'	W 101° 40.66'
71. November 22 / Up creek - good way:	N 30° 42.43'	W 101° 26.81'
72. November 23 / To mustang camp:	N 30° 42.19'	W 101° 6.89'
73. November 24 / To waterhole:	N 30° 30.63'	W 100° 53.99'

Hays/Maverick and Highsmith separate for return

74. November 25 / Hays/Maverick to SA:	N 30° 23.95'	W 100° 48.49'
75. November 26 / Down dry creek:	N 30° 12.40'	W 100° 45.29'
76. November 27 / Live oak, hills:	N 30° 2.79'	W 100° 42.10'
77. November 28 / Pretty, rich valleys:	N 29° 53.84'	W 100° 33.26'
78. November 29 / Pond W Nueces River:	N 29° 53.21'	W 100° 24.92'

79. November 30 / South captive. Philip: N 29° 42.51' W 100° 25.60'
80. December 1 / Branch W Nueces: N 29° 30.78' W 100° 23.72'
81. December 2 / Las Moras, dry creek: N 29° 16.81' W 100° 19.50'

Old Trail to San Antonio

82. December 3 / Camp 1 m W of creek: N 29° 14.32' W 100° 6.23'
83. December 4 / West bank Nueces: N 29° 12.36' W 99° 54.16'
84. December 5-6 / Leona one mile: N 29° 12.70' W 99° 46.78'
85. December 7 / Sabinal Creek: N 29° 18.87' W 99° 28.83'
86. December 8 / Seco Creek: N 29° 19.57' W 99° 17.69'
87. December 9 / Castroville: N 29° 21.32' W 98° 52.39'
88. December 10 / San Antonio: N 29° 25.58' W 98° 29.19'

Afterword

Critical Contributions to Pioneer Expedition

Several individuals or groups made critical contributions during the 1848 Pioneer Expedition, not only to successful completion of the Expedition, but also to the members' survival while exploring the terra incognita.

First, while lost in the midst of the barren canyons and hills of present-day Terrell County, Texas, the Expedition found a band of Mescalero Apaches who provided directions to Rancho San Carlos in Chihuahua, Mexico. The Mescaleros trail from Sanderson Canyon west to Fort Leaton passes through some of the most rugged, barren and dangerous terrain that one can travel by horse, canoe or vehicle in the State of Texas. Re-exploring that trail through Terrell County and the Lower Canyons of the Rio Grande confirmed how detailed as well as correct the Mescaleros information must have been.

Second, despite its being a poor village with barely enough food to feed its own people, the citizens of Rancho San Carlos, Chihuahua provided the first food, bread and milk that the men had eaten in twelve days, assuring survival until they could reach Presidio del Norte. During the days before arriving at San Carlos, the Expedition's daily diet had consisted of "tunas", Howard's "beargrass soup," tough meat from pack mules and what little could be scavenged from the barren desert lands. Once fed and "recruited" enough to travel, they rode up the Rio Grande to Fort Leaton, located a few miles below Presidio del Norte, thereby meeting one major goal, that is, finding a route along the border to Chihuahua.

Third, Ben Leaton and his associates at Fort Leaton provided the first support from Americans, including a sanctuary where the Expedition's men were safe while recovering from the extremely arduous westward exploration. Before their return to San Antonio, Ben Leaton helped Hays and Maverick find supplies and animals for the trip. If Leaton had not been able to obtain the required supplies, a return to San Antonio by Hays and the expedition would have been next to impossible. Repeated Indian depredations had removed everything of value from Presidio del Norte and the surrounding region.

Fourth, the San Miguel traders, probably "Comancheros" who traded food with Indian raiding parties for property and animals stolen in Mexico, saved the Expedition many miles of searching by confirming that no hard-bottom crossing for a wagon road existed below Horsehead Crossing. The Crossing, through which the "Upper" San Antonio-El Paso Road later passed, would be crossed for decades by thousands of migrants traveling west to California. The Pecos River near Horsehead Crossing is difficult enough to find, besides its being located in a broad, almost featureless plain. That's why the Comancheros' information about Horsehead proved to be so valuable.

Hardy Frontiersmen of Texas

Since the history of the border exploration and development of the wagon road from San Antonio to El Paso changed to military history after Lieutenant William Whiting returned to Bexar from the reconnaissance in May 1849, it is important to re-emphasize that the first two explorations of the Texas-Mexico border from Las Moras Springs (Fort Clark) to El Paso del Norte after the Treaty of Guadalupe Hidalgo as well as the search for a wagon road route were successful because of the unfailing courage and expertise of a very special group of men, Texas frontiersmen. No better recognition of their accomplishments can be given than the words of Lieutenant William H.C. Whiting with which he closed his diary.[41]

"This meager outline of our labors is now closed, but I cannot part from my brave companions without expressing here my gratitude for the resolute and un-murmuring courage with which they invariably followed and supported me, and which was equally conspicuous as well in the presence of a numerous and treacherous enemy as in enduring the privations of hunger and thirst. Skillful in the use of their arms, careful of their animals and provisions, watchful, cautious and daring, these hardy frontiersmen of Texas combine all the qualities which make the successful border soldier. For service of this kind I know none that I prefer. Well calculated as they were, however, to form an escort for Lieutenant Smith and myself on the duty assigned us, I must say that their number was far too small; and thus, while the interests dependent upon the expedition were in continual jeopardy, its objects were not as well attained as they might otherwise have been."

Despite his orders coming from General Worth, the leadership by two U.S. Army topographical engineers, and funding from the U.S. Government, Whiting's tribute to the Texas frontiersmen confirms that the 1849 reconnaissance of the Texas-Mexico was successfully completed because of the efforts of Texas frontiersmen just as the 1848 Pioneer Expedition had been. To use a modern expression, the men "with their boots on the ground" who first explored the border were not U.S. soldiers, but men who had lived and fought along Texas western frontier for many years. There is little doubt about the hardships and dangers that those early explorers overcame.

I close by recognizing their contributions with the words of Lieutenant Whiting, "For service of this kind I know none that I prefer."

References

1. Green, Rena Maverick, Editor. *Samuel Maverick, Texan: 1803–1870*. A Collection of Letters, Journals, and Memoirs. Privately published, 1952, pp. 333-342.

2. Chipman, Donald E. *Spanish Texas, 1519–1821*. Texas: University of Texas Press, 1992.

3. Howe, Daniel Walker. *What Hath God Wrought. The Transformation of America, 1815–1848*. New York: Oxford University Press, Inc, 2007, p 108.

4. Barker, Eugene C., Dodd, William E., and Commager, Henry Steele. *Our Nation's Development*. Evanston, Illinois: Row, Peterson and Company, 1934, p 240

5. Melish, John. *A Geographical Description of the United States*. Published by the Author, Philadelphia, 1816, p 32

6. Mayer, Brantz. *Mexico, Aztec, Spanish and Republican: A Historical, Geographical, Political,Statistical and Social Account of That Country From the Period of Its Invasion by the Spaniards to the Present Time*. Hartford: Volume S. Drake And Company,1852.

7. Cook, John Graham. *Jackson's Mistake: The Real and Never Before Tolld Story of Anthony Butler of South Carolina*. Acton, Massachusetts: Smashwords Edition, 2012.

8. Fehrenbach, T.R. *Lone Star. A History of Texas and the Texans*. New York: American Legacy Press, 1983 (Originally published 1968), p 174.

9. Mayer, Brantz. *Mexico As It Was and As It Is*. New York: J. Winchester, New World Press, 1844, p 339.

10. Marks, Paula Mitchell. *Turn Your Eyes Toward Texas*. Pioneers Sam and Mary Maverick. Texas A&M University Press, College Station, 1989, p 25.

11. Adams, James Truslow. *The March Of Democracy. Volume II A Half-Century of Expansion*. New York: Charles Scribner's Sons, 1932, 1933, pp 247-252.

12. May, Gary. *John Tyler*. New York: New York Times Books, 2008.

13. Borneman, Walter R. *Polk. The Man Who Transformed The Presidency and America*. New York: Random House, 2008

14. Schlarman, Joseph H.L. *MEXICO. A Land of Volcanoes. From Cortes to Aleman*. Milwaukee: The Bruce Publishing Company, 1950.

15. Meed, Douglas V. *Essential Histories. The Mexican War 1846–1848*. Oxford, UK: Osprey Publishing, 2002.

16. Griswold del Castillo, Richard. *The Treaty of Guadalupe Hidalgo. A Legacy of Conflict*. Norman, Oklahoma: University of Oklahoma Press, 1990

17. Hart, Herbert M. *Old Forts of the Southwest*. New York: Bonanza Books, 1964.

18. Wallace, Ernest, Vigness, David M., Ward, George B., Eds. *Documents of Texas History, Second Edition*. State House Press, Austin, Texas, 1994, p 23-25.

19. Weber, David J. *The Mexican Frontier 1821–1846. The American Southwest Under Mexico*. Albuquerque: University of New Mexico Press, 1982.

20. Hamalainen, Pekka. *The Comanche Empire*. New Haven: Yale University Press, 2008. (Published in Association with The William P. Clements Center for Southwest Studies, Southern Methodist University)

21. Aulbach, Louis F., Personal communication, 2003

22. Spurlin, Charles D. *Texas Veterans in the Mexican War. Muster Rolls of Texas Military Units*, Charles D. Spurlin, 1984.

23. Green, Rena Maverick, Editor. *Memoirs of Mary A. Maverick*. San Antonio: Alamo Publishing Co., 1921.

24. Bracht, Viktor. *Texas in 1848*. Translated from the German by Charles Frank Schmidt, 1931. Manchaca, Texas: German-Texan Heritage Society, 1991

25. Parker, W.B. *Through Unexplored Texas*. Notes taken during the expedition commanded by Captain R.B. Marcy, U.S.A., in the summer and fall of 1854. The Texas State Historical Association, Austin, 1990.

26. Swift, Roy L. and Corning, Leavitt, Jr. *Three Roads to Chihuahua. The Great Wagon Roads That Opened the Southwest 1823–1883*. Austin: Eakin Press, 1988.

27. Stothert, Karen E. *The Archeology and Early History of the Head of the San Antonio River*. Southern Texas Archeological Association Special Publication Number Five and Incarnate Word College Number Three, San Antonio, Texas, 1989.

28. Webb, Walter Prescott. *The Story of the Texas Rangers*. New York: Grosset & Dunlap Publishers, 1957, pp 118-119.

29. Kirkland, Forrest and Newcomb, W.W., Jr. *The Rock Art of Texas Indians*. Austin and London: University of Texas Press, 1967.

30. Chipman, Donald E. and Joseph, Harriet Denise. *Explorers and Settlers of Spanish Texas*. Austin: University of Texas, 2001.

31. McGookey, Donald P. *Geologic Wonders of West Texas*. Donald P. McGookey, Midland, Texas, 2004.

32. Press, Frank and Siever, Raymond. *Earth, Second Edition*. San Francisco: W. H. Freeman and Company, 1978, p 151.

33. Hunt, Charles B. *Natural Regions of the United States and Canada*. San Francisco: W.H. Freeman and Company, 1974, p 100.

34. Labadie, Joe H. Personal communication, 2009.

35. Jackson, A.T. *Picture-Writing of Texas Indians*. Bureau of Research in the Social Sciences, Anthropological Paper No. 27, Austin: University of Texas Press, 1938

36. Brown, John Henry. *Indian Wars and Pioneers of Texas*. Austin: L.E. Daniell, Publisher, 1880 (Re-published in 1978).

37. Aulbach, Louis F. and Butler, Joe. *The Lower Canyons of the Rio Grande*. 4th Edition, Houston, Texas: Louis F. Aulbach, 2005.

38. McGookey, Donald P., personal communication.

39. Columbia University. *EarthObserver* app for the iPad, 2012.

40. Corning, Leavitt, Jr., "The Noble Desperado of El Fortin" in *Baronial Forts of the Big Bend. Ben Leaton, Milton Faver and Their Private Forts in Presidio County*, San Antonio: Trinity University Press, 1969, pp 19-41.

41. Whiting, William H. C. *Journal of William Henry Chase Whiting, 1849* In *Exploring Southwestern Trails, 1846-1854*, Edited by Bieher, R.P. with Bender, A.B. Glendale, California: The Arthur H. Clark Company, 1938, pp 243-350.

42. Morgenthaler, Jefferson. *The River Has Never Divided Us. A Border History of La Junta de los Rios*. Austin: University of Texas Press, 2004

43. Schneider, Paul F. *Brutal Joourney. The Epic Story of the First Crossing of North America*. Henry Holt, L.L.C., 2006.

44. Weinberg, Florence Byham. *Seven Cities of Mud*. Kingsport, Tennessee: Twilight Times Books, 2008.

45. Topo! for Texas, National Geographic Maps, Evergreen, Colorado, 2003.

46. Borderwich, Fergus M. *America's Great Debate*. New York: Simon & Schuster, 2012.

47. Weddle, Robert S. San Juan Bautista. *Gateway to Spanish Texas*, Austin: University of Texas Press, (1968) 1991.

48. U.S. Congress. Senate. Reports of the Secretary of War., Reconnaissances of the Western Frontier of Texas. Orders by Geo. M. Brooke. 31st Congress, 1st session, Ex. Doc. 64, Washington, 1850, p 236.

49. U.S. Congress. Senate. Reports of the Secretary of War., Reconnaissances of Routes From San Antonio to El Paso. Report prepared by S. G. French. 31st Congress, 1st session, Ex. Doc. 64, Washington, 1850, pp 40-54.

50. Linklater, Andro. *Measuring America*. New York: Walker & Company, 2002.

51. Labadie, Joseph H. "An Overview of European History in the Amistad Basin" In Amistad National Recreation Area: A Cultural Resources Study, Labadie, J.H., Editor, National Park Service, Southwest Regional Office, Santa Fe, New Mexico, 1994.

52. West Regional Edition, Topo USAR, DeLorme. Yarmouth. ME (Versions 4.0, 5.0, 7.0), 2007

www.ingramcontent.com/pod-product-compliance
Lightning Source LLC
Chambersburg PA
CBHW020053170426
43199CB00009B/266